KU-021-540

what some of you were

stories about Christians and homosexuality

what some of you were

stories about
Christians and homosexuality

edited by Christopher Keane

Liberty Christian Ministries

MATTHIAS MEDIA

What Some of You Were
© Matthias Media, 2001

Published in the United Kingdom by:
The Good Book Company
Tel: 0845 225 0880
email: admin@thegoodbook.co.uk
website: www.thegoodbook.co.uk

Unless otherwise indicated, Scripture taken from the HOLY BIBLE, NEW
INTERNATIONAL VERSION. Copyright © 1973, 1978, 1984 International
Bible Society. Used by permission of Zondervan Bible Publishers.

ISBN 1 876326 41 7

Cover design and typesetting by Joy Lankshear Design
Printed in China

*Do you not know that the wicked will
not inherit the kingdom of God?
Do not be deceived: Neither the sexually
immoral nor idolaters nor adulterers
nor male prostitutes nor homosexual
offenders nor thieves nor the greedy nor
drunkards nor slanderers nor swindlers
will inherit the kingdom of God.
And that is what some of you were.
But you were washed, you were
sanctified, you were justified in the
name of the Lord Jesus Christ and by
the Spirit of our God.*

1 Corinthians 6:9-11

Preface

*D*espite what the secular media and the gay community say, there are many Christians who do not wish to embrace a gay identity. These are people who, because of their commitment to Jesus Christ and their belief in the Bible, choose not to act upon their same-sex attraction.

Many, because of the shame involved for them or because of past hurts, will not disclose this in their own church. They prefer to go outside the familiar environment of their church fellowship for support. But where do these people go? Liberty Christian Ministries Inc. exists to provide a safe place for Christians who are seeking support in their choice.

Liberty doesn't talk people out of homosexuality. We don't proselytize the gay community. We believe that people have the right to make their own choices for their lives. If they wish to be actively homosexual, that is their business. If their choice is to live a life according to their Christian convictions, that also is their business and that choice deserves to be respected and supported.

In the following pages you will have the privilege of reading the stories of people, all known to us, who have made that choice. They wish to share their struggles and the way in which

God has brought about change in their lives. Their hope is that these stories will serve to:

• bring encouragement and hope to those who are also struggling with unwanted feelings of same-sex attraction;

• educate, inform and encourage the wider Christian community about how to respond to homosexuality, and in particular how to help those in our midst who are struggling.

We have also included stories of people who have been affected by the homosexuality (and in one case, the transsexuality) of a person close to them.

All the stories are only as current as when they were given to us. Peoples' names have been changed to protect their privacy. The text of this book has not been edited heavily—these are the real words of real people, each of them on a journey. We have not tried to iron out their theology, or put words in their mouths.

Many people are confused by homosexuality, so we have included some articles which will hopefully shed light on this complex issue from a Christian perspective. It is our desire and prayer that this book will enlighten and help you in your thinking about the subject of homosexuality.

Christopher Keane

See 'Contact details' at the end of this book for how to contact Liberty or similar ministries around Australia and the rest of the world.

Table of Contents

What some of you were 11
    Edward Vaughan

Our Stories

Christopher 17

Ann 31

Jack 37

Emma 43

Dazza 49

Robin 57

Mother

What it's like to be the mother of a transsexual 63

The story of Jane: a mother's perspective 69

Daughter

Audrey 79

Wife

Laura 85

Sara 91

Together

Revelation and recovery: a wife's story 97

Learning a new way: a husband's story 105

Notes 115

Appendices

1. How we went gay 119
    Tony Payne

2. Is homosexuality biologically determined? 135
    Dr Trevor Hunter

3. On homosexuality and change 145
    Dr Trevor Hunter

4. Homosexuality in the New Testament 153
    Glenn N. Davies

Contact details 167

Study Guide 169

What some of you were...

Edward Vaughan

It was just before the Mardi Gras one year. I was driving in my car listening to talkback radio. I listened as a spokesman for the Mardi Gras said, "It's a celebration of love, creativity and human sexuality. Being gay is just another way to be human, to be a family, to be together". He spoke with the voice of common-sense, the voice of reason.

Then the lines were opened to those who wished to comment. The callers fell into two categories. One group agreed with the spokesman, and also spoke with the same voice of reason. As for the other group—it was rabid, bigoted, angry, aggressive, simply embarrassing, often misinformed. And often claiming to be Christian.

I reached over and turned off the radio with a deep sense of despair. I seemed to have only two options—to affirm homosexuality as a lifestyle choice, as acceptable as any other, or to be narrow-minded and hateful.

It doesn't seem like much of a choice to me.

The part of Scripture that has shaped my view on homosexuality is the parable of the Pharisee and the Tax Collector (Luke 18:9-14). A bit surprising, perhaps, because it doesn't mention homosexuality at all.

Jesus addresses the story to "some who were confident of their own righteousness, and looked down on everyone else". As so often in the hands of Jesus, the parable is an attack weapon, a subversive and offensive story. Who is forgiven by God? The good man or the scumbag tax collector? To our shock, it is the sinner, the one who knows he struggles and cries out to God in humility.

If you are a fine moral upright person—watch out! You are in Pharisee country! Christ's people are sinners in search of mercy.

Jesus taught forgiveness, but he also taught repentance. And we all need to repent, especially of our acts of homophobia. I was reflecting recently on a suburban church of which I was once a member. In that church, I think it would have been impossible for an adolescent in our fellowship to come out and say "I think I'm gay". We didn't create a safe place for people to be honest about their struggles. We allowed a culture of fear, where being honest would have meant almost certain rejection and ridicule.

In that church, I think *we* were guilty of sin. The Bible is not homophobic. God is not a persecutor of homosexuals, and his people know only too well the depths of their failure before him. It's very hard to be violent to someone when you are looking them in the eyes with your hand around their shoulder saying, "I have sinned too".

Look at Leviticus 18. Run your eye down the passage. It's a list of sexual practices that are unacceptable to God. You will note that homosexuality is included, along with a range of other practices.

We cannot walk away from this. But let's make it clear. The Bible does not say, "Straight sex is good, gay sex is bad". Heterosexual adultery is no more and no less of a sin than homosexuality. Christians do not argue for heterosexuality, but for obedience to God. That has implications for all of us, no matter what our gender orientation.

And we must be clear about this. There is a difference between saying homosexuality is unacceptable to God and being homophobic. When one says the Bible stands against adultery, one is not regarded as heterophobic. When one says the Bible stands against the performance of homosexual acts, that is not homophobic. It is not vilification to say that God rejects some human sexual behaviour. And it is no more homophobic than rejecting Christ and his messengers is Christophobic.

Paul condemns a range of human behaviours (1 Corinthians 6:9-11). Homosexuality is on the list, alongside drunkenness and greed. Paul does not suggest one is better or worse than the other—these kinds of actions are incompatible with being the people of God.

But the part I love is verse 11—"That is what some of you were...". From the very beginning the church of Christ has been made up of people who were substance abusers, adulterers, liars, compulsive spenders—and homosexuals. The church is made up of people who have found mercy in Christ.

No matter who I am or what I have done, I am a candidate for regeneration in Christ. Praise God that he should have mercy on a sinner like me.

Our Stories

Christopher

My introduction to homosexuality came about through someone in my church. I became a Christian when I was sixteen, and had been attending a local church since my conversion. I had a strong desire to know God. I loved the Bible and I was learning about prayer. I was growing in my relationship with God and it was all pretty exciting. Although I was attracted sexually to other men, it wasn't something I was going to bring up at the Wednesday night prayer meeting.

An older man started attending our church. I had an instinct about this man, and it wasn't long before we both knew we were attracted to each other, and a relationship began.

I knew enough to realise that, for me, Christianity and active homosexuality were not a compatible mix. I suppose there were three choices I could have made. Firstly, I could have fought the temptation and continued with Christianity. Or I could have gone into the relationship and continued to attend church. But my choice was to leave God and to enter into what I hoped would be a lifelong, faithful relationship.

The relationship ended after a few months, and some of the gay people I had met introduced me to the bar and pub scene which was part of the gay lifestyle in Sydney in the sixties.

At first my involvement in the gay lifestyle was exciting. I was young, many of the people were sophisticated and interesting, and I was receiving lots of attention from older men—attention I had never had from my father.

The lifestyle was also very seductive. The same-sex attraction I had been aware of before was now out in the open, and I was involved in a group where this was normal. Instead of feeling I had to *hide* my homosexuality, it was now a relief to be with this group where I fitted in because I *was* homosexual.

But the most important thing for me was the possibility of finding the long-term faithful relationship I had always so desperately wanted. My desire was to meet 'Mr Right' and settle down where all my needs were going to be met by this 'Prince Charming'.

I was part of the gay community for fifteen years, and during that time I had four relationships. These were not the loving, stable, monogamous, 'happy-ever-after' relationships I had wanted. They were dysfunctional, destructive and damaging. After the demise of my fourth relationship, I seriously began to question my involvement with homosexuality.

I knew that morally it was not right for me. I had never lost my awareness of God, and I knew the day would come when I would have to sort out my relationship with him.

I was now beginning to question seriously much of the gay propaganda which I had believed, especially the myth of the stable, faithful, long-term relationship. I was looking closely at many of the people with whom I mixed, and I was beginning to realise how seriously damaged some of them were. I was also realistic enough to know there was damage in my own life. I was well aware of the alarmingly high abuse of drugs and alcohol in the gay scene, and I had begun to abuse these substances myself. I was acutely conscious of how unhappy I was. Although I owned my own apartment, had an excellent job and as much money as I needed, when I took a good look at it, my life was a mess. I was now at the point of being completely disillusioned. It had taken me fifteen years to come to the realization that homosexuality was not working for me, so I decided to get out.

The only positive thing I had learned from my experience was that I now knew beyond any shadow of doubt there was nothing that lifestyle had to offer me.

The first thing I did after I left the gay community was to recommit my life to Jesus Christ. I gave him as much of myself as I could at first. Later, as my trust in him deepened, I gave him more. As far as I could at that time, I made a decision to trust him.

I wish I could say once I had done all of that I lived happily ever after, but I can't. In leaving the homosexual community, I left an entire culture. For example, it had its own dress codes, vocabulary, entertainers, music, humour and morality. I went into the church community and it had its own culture, dress code, vocabulary, music and moral code. Obviously this was a huge adjustment, and there was a lot of change and grief involved.

I was grieving over the loss of the lifestyle and some of the friends I had left. While I had no regrets about leaving the gay culture, I was missing some of the people I had been close to. I felt that if I had opened up about this at church, I probably would not have been understood.

There was also a big adjustment to the culture of the church. Everything was different and it took time to get used to the very different environment I had joined. I had come from the hectic, fast paced and at times bizarre homosexual culture, into the very sheltered and unworldly atmosphere of the church. Even getting used to the radically different way people expressed themselves was at times strange, and there were times when I felt we were speaking a different language. One day someone prayed for a couple who were going on holidays. They asked God for "journeying mercies" for this couple. What on earth were "journeying mercies"? I wondered. The only thing I could think of was clean toilets on the way to wherever they were going!

I was now celibate after being sexually active for many years, and I found that difficult at times. I was also attempting to make a new set of friends, as I'd cut my ties with all my former acquaintances. I was learning to relate to heterosexual men—I'd never had a problem relating to women—and at times just finding things I had in common with the men in the church was difficult, as I had never been interested in sport or any of what is traditionally regarded as 'male interests'. There were other things going on at that time as well. I had never dealt with any of the past hurts in my life. Now I found God was raising issues I needed to give some attention to.

At about the age of three or four I had been abused by an uncle, and I had never dealt with the effects of that abuse. I was also still carrying a lot of hurts experienced in the four failed gay relationships, and I had never really dealt with the grief involved in these break-ups. I was slowly becoming aware of the emotional deprivation I had experienced as a child. I can never remember my father showing me any affection. He certainly never seemed interested in me, or spent any time with me. Consequently, learning about God's fatherly love for me was very difficult as I had no experience to use as a model.

It would have been helpful at that time to have had someone to talk with about some of these things. Someone who knew how to listen, who was understanding and accepting. This would have reduced my isolation, speeded up my recovery and supported me in the process I was going through.

Over many years, I went on to deal with a whole lot of things, including what I now see as the roots of my homosex-

uality. These were my childhood abuse, the emotional detachment from my father, emotional deprivation, rejection, and
external labelling or name-calling

Labelling had been a very destructive thing for me, as I will
explain. School was a lonely and painful time of my life.
Although I had some friendships, there was a lot of name-calling or 'labelling' (poofter, pansy, queer), as I was effeminate
and different from most of the other kids. This was not very
surprising, seeing I had not had a healthy masculine role
model in my family, and had modelled on my sisters. To deal
with this labelling I had to be willing to forgive the people
who had called me names. This was a process, and like any
process, it took time.

I used many different means to deal with the things I
believed God was showing me. I attended a lot of secular self-
development groups. When I was eventually brave enough
to confide in Christians, I had prayer ministry and also professional counselling. I spent hours reading and praying
through the Bible, as well as any other books I thought would
be helpful. Whatever was available, I used.

Over many years, as the roots of my homosexuality were
dealt with thoroughly, and with God, I realized an amazing
thing. I became aware that my sexual responses were changing.

I first became aware of this one day when I had decided to
attend a service in another denomination. As I was waiting for
the service to begin, I noticed a young woman sitting a couple of
rows ahead of me. I sat there admiring her. She was a stunning-
looking girl. Beautiful skin, lovely hair, and there was a purity
about her that I had never seen in any of the men in the gay culture. As I sat staring at this young woman, I became aware that
my response to her had quite a large sexual component to it.

I had to think through the ramifications of what had happened. One of the myths I had accepted was 'once gay, always gay, you're born that way'. My experience of responding to that girl in church had proved that to be wrong! I was also aware that for a long time, I had not been attracted to men in a sexual way. I now had to admit to myself that my sexuality was far from fixed—it was changing, and that was quite a revelation to me. I had to re-think all that I had accepted and believed up to that time. This was difficult, as there was no-one I could talk to, nor were there any books that I was aware of that would have helped me to do this.

Also helpful in my process were my friendships with other Christian men. I spent time with these men, and learned to relate to them in ways that were healthy. We shared with each other, listened to each other and prayed together. Apart from friendship, these guys provided me with the good role models I needed, as my father hadn't provided for me in that way. The relationships were firmly based on mutuality. None of these men treated me as their 'project'. I would have found this extremely offensive, and no relationship would have been possible if they had attempted to make me a 'good deed'. I wanted friendship and respect as a person; I did not want to be patronized and paraded as a 'good work'.

It's been a long, and at times very painful road of growth and change for me, but the blessings have far outweighed any pain I have experienced. One of the blessings has been a change in my sexual responses, and from that change has come a wonderful marriage.

The marriage came *after* the change in my sexuality, not before. It is very important that people realise that marriage will *not* change them. We all bring our emotional baggage and the damage that has caused into our marriages with us, and I am very grateful that the bulk of mine was well and truly dealt with before I married.

Well, that's my story, but some of you may still ask, "What about other homosexuals? Is change *really possible* for them? And what exactly do you mean by 'change'? Is every one who deals with their same-sex desires going to end up with changed sexual responses and possibly married?".

No, of course they're not.

Joe Dallas is a man who has come out of homosexuality, and he has worked in ex-gay ministry for many years. In his book *Desires in Conflict*, he addresses the person who struggles with unwanted homosexual desires and says:

> If you are motivated and willing to exercise patience and discipline, you have good reason to be optimistic about change... Change does not occur quickly. In fact, it happens so gradually that you may hardly notice it at first... change occurs to different degrees among different people. Some claim complete conversion of sexual desire from homosexual to heterosexual. Others experience reduction, not absence, of homosexual attractions. Still others allow that, although they are no longer aroused by their own sex, they could backslide or regress to homosexual attractions.[1]*

There are voices within some of our churches that would opt for acceptance of homosexuality as a valid alternative lifestyle, and I'd like to comment on that. Some parts of the church say that we should bless those homosexuals who are in a loving, faithful union.

John Stott, in his book *New Issues Facing Christians Today*, says:

> The concept of lifelong, quasi-marital fidelity in homosexual partnerships is largely a myth, a theoretical ideal

Notes are found on p.115.

which is contradicted by the facts. The truth is that gay relationships are characterized more by promiscuity than by fidelity (p. 402).[2]

A good example of this is found in Joseph Nicolosi's book *Reparative Therapy Of Male Homosexuality*. He says:

...in 1984, McWhirter and Mattison published "The Male Couple", an in-depth study designed to evaluate the quality and stability of long-term homosexual couplings. Their study was undertaken to disprove the reputation that male relationships do not last. The authors themselves are a homosexual couple, one a psychiatrist, the other a psychologist. After much searching they were able to locate 156 male couples in relationships that had lasted from 1 to 37 years. Two-thirds of the respondents had entered the relationship with either the implicit or the explicit expectation of sexual fidelity. The results show that of those 156 couples, only seven had been able to maintain sexual fidelity. Furthermore, of those seven couples, none had been together more than five years. In other words, the researchers were unable to find a single male couple that was able to maintain sexual fidelity for more than five years.

The authors added: "The expectation for outside sexual activity was the rule for male couples and the exception for heterosexuals."[3]

After spending fifteen years in the lifestyle, my own experience confirms the findings of McWhirter and Mattison.

Just before I came out of homosexuality, a friend and I sat down one Saturday afternoon, and had a very sad but enlightening conversation. We came to the conclusion that we knew no-one who was in a faithful relationship. The couples we knew had sex with others as well as their partners. Often the partners knew about the infidelity, but sometimes they didn't. Some of these couples had group sex or anonymous sex in public toilets or bathhouses. We could think of no-one we knew who was in a faithful relationship. We had both been active homosexuals for fifteen years, and we came to the conclusion that afternoon that between us we had spent thirty years chasing something which just did not exist. That day was the beginning of the end of homosexuality for me.

Thomas Schmidt, author of *Straight and Narrow*, sums it up well when he says:

> Promiscuity among homosexual men is not a mere stereotype, and it is not merely the majority experience— it is virtually the *only* experience...In short, there is practically no comparison possible to heterosexual marriage in terms of either fidelity or longevity. Tragically, lifelong faithfulness is almost non-existent in the homosexual experience.[4]

As I have already said, this was my life experience for fifteen years.

I chose to leave the gay culture. There are many Christians who have chosen not to be involved in it at all.

For some of these people, celibacy will be their choice, as it is for many heterosexuals. Others will pursue a change in their sexual responses. Whatever they choose, their choice not to identify with, or to be a part of, the homosexual community needs to be respected and supported by the church.

How can churches make it easier for the Christians who struggle with same-sex desires, but choose not to embrace a gay identity?

First, we need to realise that discussion of homosexuality often raises strong feelings. It is painful for those who are affected by it, it invokes anger for those who are offended by the 'in your face' attitude of the gay community, and in many cases it engenders fear and confusion for those who are uninformed.

I think it's helpful if we try to see homosexuality as a two-sided coin.

On one side, we have the gay community, which includes those who have chosen homosexuality as their lifestyle. Some of these people are angry and militant. There are also many in the gay community who have been hurt by the church and feel that they have no place in the body of Christ. This belief would be enforced by the behaviour of some Christians, as well as what the media says about the church's attitude to homosexuality.

On the other side of the coin, we have the many Christians who are struggling with an unwanted same-sex attraction, in an environment (the church) which, for the most part, doesn't understand—and in some cases doesn't want to understand—the condition or the process involved for those who want change.

I believe that if the church wants to be an effective and helpful part of the change process, there are many within it who need to deal with their fear of homosexuality, and educate themselves about the subject. Many Christians are confused and disgusted by homosexuality, and unfortunately there are many who have incorporated their prejudices into their theology.

In the preface of his book *Same Sex Partnerships*, John Stott says, "[i]s there a Christian way to combine biblical thinking about God's intention for human sexuality with an equally biblical attitude of understanding, respect and support for persons with a homosexual disposition?".[5]

I believe there is.

So how do we go about it?

1) Respect the authority of Scripture

We must not rewrite or water down the Scriptures. The Bible clearly states that heterosexuality is God's intent for humanity. It presents all sexual behaviour outside of marriage as sin, and not God's best for us. When I came out of the gay community, I was looking for truth and direction. My friends said I was a fool. My perception of the church at that time was that they could only put homosexual people down and had no idea of how to assist in the process of recovery. I found direction from the Bible. It was the Bible that gave me a true picture of God as a Father, and of his unconditional love for all his children, regardless of their struggles. I found through the Scriptures that God cared about me and loved me. I learned healthy boundaries for living, from reading the Bible. It was there that I learned the things I needed in order to function in a whole way. While the Bible didn't 'cure' me, it gave me the grounding I needed when I moved forward to counselling.

I shudder to think what may have happened to me if I had gone to a counsellor (or to a church) who had not upheld the Scriptures and had affirmed me in my homosexuality. If that had happened I may well have been dead from AIDS now. Many of the people I knew when I was part of the gay community are now dead.

2) We need to uphold one standard

I am constantly amazed at the double standards within the church. As Earl Wilson says in his book *Counselling and Homosexuality*:

> We believe that lying is a sin, yet we reach out to liars. We believe that adultery is a sin and find compassion

for the adulterer. We believe that the practice of homosexuality is a sin and close our doors to both the pras-
ticing homosexual and the person who is trying hard to
obey God.[6]

He goes on to say, "We can't help the hurting or bring life to
those who need God when they only feel our rejection".

Some people seem to put homosexuality in the 'worst sin'
category even though the Bible doesn't do that. Before we start
judging the homosexual, we may need to look at our own
lives. Do we watch R-rated movies? Do we fantasize over the
girls (or the boys) in the office? Do we enjoy a little pornography? If we can say 'yes' to these questions, do we *really* think
our sin is more acceptable to God because it's heterosexual? If
there are people who do think that way, they have a very pecu-
liar belief system, which is certainly not biblical.

3) We must provide for people

With a little commonsense and thoughtfulness, any church can
begin to help people who struggle in this area. Listening with
sensitivity, providing educational opportunities or material,
keeping a list of reliable Christian counsellors at hand for the
people who may need them, and even providing a supportive
setting for people in need, are all possible options.

It may mean reading and learning more about homosexuality, and asking God to help us to deal with any fears and prejudices we have about homosexuality. It may also mean telling
people that jokes and put-downs about homosexuality are inappropriate.

During my many years of involvement in the church since I
left the gay community, I have realized just how widespread the

problem of homosexuality is within the Christian community. Sadly, I have also realized just how ill-equipped, and sometimes unwilling, the church is to deal with it. The ignorance about the subject is frightening. Take for example the man who was told that if he married, his homosexuality would disappear. Or the person who was told what was really needed was a simple deliverance from the 'demon' of homosexuality. Women have been told that if they looked more feminine, wore lipstick and dresses and found themselves a virile male (even though many have been sexually abused by men), they would not have a sexuality problem. But perhaps the award for absurdity should go to the person who said homosexuality was caused by people eating Kentucky Fried Chicken. This person believed it was the female hormones fed to the chickens that were the cause of homosexuality.

Let's sum up the points that I have given you as a way forward for Christian churches.

1) We need to respect the authority of Scripture.

2) We need to uphold one standard.

3) We need to provide for people.

We need to beware of thinking we are better than the person who struggles with homosexuality. We're not. Christianity is a great leveller, isn't it? I'm ex-gay, but as Christians we are all ex-something.

Sy Rogers[7] once said, "It's not heterosexuality that gets us a ticket to heaven, it's a relationship with Jesus".

If you are struggling with homosexuality I want to say this to you: There *is* hope and healing for you as you deal with your unwanted homosexual feelings. You are not a second-class Christian because you struggle with this. Jesus' death was for you as well. *You are not an unwanted child.* God is not ashamed of you. He is your Father and longs to lavish his love, forgiveness and care on you.

If you are struggling with homosexuality or any other problem in your life, I would like to suggest to you that the best place to begin dealing with that problem is with Jesus. For me, it started with forgiveness and turning away from my past life. From there Jesus took me on a journey of change and healing, for which I will always be grateful.

Ann

*H*aving been a regular Anglican church-goer for just about all of my 52 years, I was well acquainted with the *Southern Cross* monthly newsletter. Through the October 1996 edition, I first learnt of the work of Liberty Christian Ministries Inc. The effect of the article was like bells ringing. I realized there was help for those who struggled with unwanted homosexual feelings, not only of a sexual nature but where emotional dependency, co-dependency and/or relationship addiction were very much part of one's make-up—in short, for people like me.

I hesitated—me, asking for support? Wasn't that an admission of failure? I thought long and hard, then discussed it with a good friend whom I trusted, and whose judgement I trusted. The upshot was that I realized I had nothing to lose, and a lot to gain. So I took the plunge, and a fortnight later attended my first support session. I was so nervous I was shaking. That session was the first of many others over the next year. Those sessions led me to a fresh start, and a different perspective on life—and me.

Some months earlier, I had seen a review in *Southern Cross* of Briar Whitehead's book *Craving For Love.*[8] I bought the

WHAT SOME OF YOU WERE

book—what an eye-opener! For the first time, I had hope that I could change. However, I really needed support and help, and I found both when I learned about the work of Liberty.

Looking back on my life, I did not have many male friends. I was extremely shy, and found mixing with the opposite sex difficult. Strangely, I had been an absolute tomboy growing up. My brother and I were very competitive, and the backyard was often the scene for aggressive games of cricket and soccer, with neighbourhood boys usually joining in. My brother was a few years older than me, but I never stopped trying to prove that I was as good as he was.

The men I went out with more than once could be counted on the fingers of one hand. There were, however, two with whom I did go out for a reasonable length of time, one for three months and the other for a year. It was I who broke off the friendships—I just could not feel at ease with them. They were both fine men, but I shrank from any type of physical touch.

I never lacked female friends. Most were normal, sound friendships. A few were intense and there were two where I became sexually involved. The first relationship lasted for about four years. The second came four years later, and there was a lot of trauma involved until I achieved the break a year later. I never lived with either of these women, as I still lived with my parents at that time, so the relationships were intermittent. But they happened, and the guilt stayed with me long after.

As far as my spiritual life was concerned, I had started Sunday School when I was three, attended regularly until I was fifteen, then became a teacher for eight years and also joined the church choir. My faith played a big part in my life—I loved the church. I still do.

But my emotional problems caused a lot of heartache within. I craved affection and yet I couldn't find it in the appropriate, God-given way. I felt an absolute misfit.

So to my first session and the start of an intense thirst for knowledge. I read and read—books, newsletters, leaflets—and I listened to tapes. There seemed to be messages for me in almost everything I touched, all recommended by my supporters. I found that any message of special import had greater impact if I wrote it down—I wrote reams! I also started to read the Bible again but in a new way. I found the NIV the most helpful, and the "Day By Day" devotional books the most illuminating.

At each support session, I would discuss my findings and we would work through the various issues. Gradually I learnt why I 'ticked' the way I did. My supporters prayed for me. Such prayers I had not heard before. They were uplifting and soul-restoring, full of encouragement and joy in my progress. God was indeed good to me.

For me, this help came at the right time and was given by the right people. Two big changes in my life had occurred. Firstly, after 34 years in a government department, I had opted for voluntary redundancy. And the second great change was even more important: my father died. My mother, though independent, was 85 and needed help that I could not have given had I continued to work full-time. I just knew I was meant to leave the Department. It was timely—God's time, as I came to realise. His hand was truly guiding me. Also, without this time I could never have dealt with the issues I was now dealing with. Ecclesiastes has it right: "There is a time for everything, and a season for every activity under heaven" (3:1).

To reveal my innermost feelings to perfect strangers made me cringe at first. I felt so vulnerable and ashamed, yet I knew that what was happening was important. The love, care and total acceptance I received from my supporters truly warmed my heart. A rapport quickly developed and so did friendship.

They were also good role models. They had had their own problems, but had come through the "refining fire". They were a living testament to God's grace and to the reality that God can change us and lead us to complete wholeness.

As I said earlier, I had fallen sexually with two people. But since then I had had no involvement with anyone for 21 years, knowing in my heart that such relationships were contrary to God's will. Yet I knew I still had problems. At my first session, I was given a copy of a newsletter on emotional dependency. Boy, did I learn heaps about myself from that newsletter! I realized I was emotionally dependent on three of my friends and that those friendships were too intense. I learnt from subsequent sessions, and from reading, that codependency and relationship addiction had also been very much part of me and were interrelated.

Like all of us, some of my problems were rooted in child-hood. I came from a very undemonstrative family. I had English ancestry and the English reserve was very evident in my family. It didn't help my feelings of isolation and estrangement. My brother always seemed to be the favourite. He was an extrovert, and performed well academically and at sport. I was very much an introvert (made worse by a moderate hearing loss), and although I was also good at sport, I was, in terms of exams, less of a performer at schoolwork. My mother especially could not understand why this was so, and made my life hell at exam-time to the point where I dreaded going home. I also remember her saying to me that I should be more like my brother, and the hurt of that stayed with me for years. The eternal question in my heart was, "Why can't you accept me as I am?".

There were many such hurts during my childhood and teenage years. I think now that my mother was well-inten-tioned, but found my brother easier to handle. My father was a gentleman of the old school and saw his role as the protector and bread-winner. I was always a child to him, even in later years, long after I had left the family home. He was a caring man, full of integrity and with a strong sense of responsibility and duty. I always thought he favoured my brother, partly because of his personality, but also simply because he was male and probably therefore found it easier to relate to him.

I am happy to say that after I left home to live alone nearby, the relationship with my parents improved. In more recent years, as they became older and less independent, they both valued my contribution and assistance. Unfortunately, the damage had been done early in life and the scars remained. Reading over what I have written about my parents, I have feelings of guilt and disloyalty, but they are my perceptions of that time and those perceptions affected me deeply.

Over the past year I have learned to accept myself. I have realized that I am special, and uniquely me. I am worthwhile and loved by God. I have learned to forgive myself, where in the past I was hard on myself. I have also learned to be able to forgive others, those who have hurt me unwittingly or otherwise. A verse of Scripture that has been very special to me through this year of change and growth is Zephaniah 3:17. "The Lord your God is with you, he is mighty to save. He will take great delight in you, he will quiet you with his love, he will rejoice over you with singing." I have learned to rejoice in my femininity. I have learned how complementary the relationship between a man and a woman can be. I have also learned a bit about what makes men tick. I always regarded them as from another planet, but am now relieved to find that they live on earth too!

I have also learned a lot about prayer. Before, this had been an area much lacking in my spiritual life. I have come to realize that prayer can mean just listening and simply being in God's presence, rather than forever bombarding him with petitions in a perfunctory sort of way. But it can also be really pouring out my problems, worries and fears and letting him deal with them rather than getting in his way.

There have been beautiful times when I would see images, or hear God speaking to me. Once I could see Jesus walking beside me, taking me by the hand along life's road—I still see that scene. Another time when some personal problems seemed overwhelming, I heard him say, "Lean on me". In the past I wouldn't give him the time to give me these messages, I was too busy rushing through my prayers to listen!

All the way through my support sessions I recorded my thoughts, as well as any Bible verses that struck me like neon lights—in fact, anything and everything that helped me in my progress. This has helped me to retrace my steps and see my triumphs as well as my pitfalls. I found re-reading what I have written quite astounding. Some areas of my life need more work, but in other areas I have come through "the refining fire". I now have a contentment and a peace that has never existed before. I am comfortable with myself. My self-esteem is healthier, and I no longer place my friends on pedestals. I have expanded my group of friends and no longer look to one or two 'exclusive' friendships to meet my needs—in other words, I no longer put all my eggs in one basket. I still have some problems saying 'no' to people, and I can run myself ragged at times. Reading the book *Boundaries* by Dr Henry Cloud and Dr John Townsend has helped me to improve in this area.[9] There are still times when I hate not being in control, but I am working on this.

At first when it was suggested to me to write my story, I baulked—I didn't think I was ready. But I have finally decided to write it as a traveller who has come some distance. I am on the way, and God is with me.

Jack

I share my story knowing that it is not a 'before and after' inspiring tale, or even one that proffers a happy conclusion. In truth, I feel I am on a journey, and I am uncertain how it will end. Yet it is my story, and one where God's hand has been at work.

I was brought up in an average middle-class home in the suburbs, the child of baby boomers. My father served in the defence forces and during my early years was often away, leaving my mother to manage young children and a full-time job as best she could. This arrangement continued until I started school, when my father left the services and took up work in an adjacent suburb.

My family were not Christians, though my best friend at primary school was. During my growing years I spent a great deal of time at my friend's house and related well to that family.

I found my father, while a good and kind man, remote and emotionally distant. His strongest emotion was released after drinking copious quantities of alcohol, and that emotion was anger. Although I never felt at physical risk in his presence, my strongest reaction toward him was fear. I felt at times he didn't know how to show love to us, and that caused him great frustration, boiling over after he drank. It was to be twenty years before I learned that he himself had never been fathered. His father left him and his mother when Dad was ten years old, to fight in a war that he never returned from. My father had no siblings.

Nevertheless, my childhood was filled with exploration and adventures, for we lived quite near a national park, and my growing years were remarkable only for my increasing curiosity about God. I used to pray regularly, although I didn't know what I should pray for, or even if God would hear me. My best friend's family were church attenders and so I started going to church with them, as well as joining Sunday School and enjoying day outings and camps. It was at one of these camps that I heard of Jesus Christ and his death for me. When asked to respond, I did, and committed my life to Christ. I was about 11 years old at the time.

From that time on I increased my involvement at church, eventually joining a youth group led by a dynamic and capable leader whom I greatly admired. As I entered adolescence, I became aware of an increasing admiration for, and strong emotional response towards, the athletic boys in my class at school. My talents lay more in the intellectual sphere rather than with physical prowess. Since the former was not valued, I felt constantly inferior and longed to be like the boys I held in awe. I used to shake when near them and it would make my day if one even noticed me, let alone spoke to me.

I once spoke to my youth leader about these feelings. He informed me that these were homosexual feelings and that perhaps that is what I was. Our relationship changed and he began to spend more time with me. I felt a desperate need to talk, and he was a sympathetic ear.

Late one night after an intense discussion in his car, he laid his hand on my knee and invited me to have sex with him. I felt confused and refused his offer. He persisted in asking, but eventually he gave up and took me home. I should have been disgusted and angry, yet I felt neither emotion. After deciding to tell no-one what had happened, I continued to attend the youth group led by this man. He is now an acknowledged and respected Christian leader. At the time, I was going out with a girl in my year at school. We were emotionally close, yet this had not been expressed physically. In my recollection, one final event took place that led me to abandon all efforts at heterosexual relationships.

One hot summer's night my family had a BBQ in our back yard. On this occasion my father had drunk even more than his usual large quantity of alcohol. He invited me to sit with him. In a strident and angry voice he described graphically the nature of heterosexual intercourse and the risks of pregnancy and sexually transmitted disease. I felt physically ill, and terrified as he spoke. At the time I was a mid-adolescent who had barely held a girl's hand, let alone thought to behave as he was intimating. Many decades later I confronted him over the events of that night though he had no memory of them. He did relate that when serving overseas, his job was to take the young recruits and explain to them the risks of engaging in sexual behaviour with the indigenous female population. He said his strategy was intended to scare them into taking precautions. At nineteen or twenty this message would have been disturbing—to me, it was terrifying. The following weekend when my girlfriend tried to kiss me, I fled her house and never spoke to her again.

I finished my studies and turned to work, there meeting and enjoying the company of females, especially over late-night coffee. Usually there would come the opportunity to allow the relationship to develop emotionally and physically, and on each occasion I would terminate the relationship rather than deal with the fear and anxiety I was experiencing. I had no such qualms with males, though most did not long to be close to me in the way I wanted closeness with them.

I had assumed responsibilities in my church, and was recognized as an able teacher and leader of youth. This brought me into contact with many young men of attractive looks and athletic ability whom I deeply admired. I was available to all the youth in my groups, yet I especially found time to spend with these young men. The Lord was merciful and used me powerfully in these peoples' lives. A number are now serving the Lord overseas and in Australia in significant areas of ministry.

As my hunger for intimacy grew, so did my preparedness to take risks. I ingratiated myself with one young man and his family, and eventually my relationship with him reached such a level of intimacy that I invited him to sleep with me. He declined and burst into tears. I felt such a level of shame and disgust at how things had come full circle, that even now, more than a decade later, that emotional memory is painful.

Over these years I sought help from a number of professional sources without much benefit—though the insights I gained have helped me piece together the story that I am relating to you.

I decided that the answer for me would not be found in therapy, but in the attractive and welcoming arms of the gay community. I had a Christian friend who persuaded me that this was God's purpose for my life—that I stop hiding my homosexuality; instead that I freely express it and seek affirmation for it. The next two years flew by in a haze of gay bars, parties and social outings. My friends and I were visual addicts—we sought out the most handsome and available male in each context, then tried to monopolize his time and his attention, even if that meant thwarting others' efforts to be noticed. Bitter sarcasm and recriminations would flow when we all lost out, as was usually the case. Rather than question what we were doing, we would simply try harder the next time.

Eventually I found someone, and a relationship was on offer. This would be the first time for me, and I was determined to give myself over to it. However, I continued to read Scripture and seek God's blessing over the direction my life was about to take.

One night I read the words of John 5:39-40, where Jesus addressed the Pharisees of his day. "You diligently study the Scriptures because you think that by them you possess eternal life. These are the Scriptures that testify about me, yet you refuse to come to me to have life."

As I read these words, I sensed Jesus was now speaking directly to me. He was angry with me and seemed to say: "You have gone everywhere with this issue except to me. You bring this issue directly to me and lay it at my feet. Don't you dare go anywhere else with it. I HAVE DIED FOR YOU, AND MY DEATH IS SUFFICIENT EVEN FOR THIS".

In my pain I cried out, "I have to go this way because it's who I am—I only know myself as gay".

He replied, "But this is not how I know you; therefore, your knowledge of yourself as gay is false".

It felt like the rug had been pulled out from under my feet. For many days I felt in free fall. I would wake up in the morning and though my bedroom faces east I couldn't see the sun, despite it having risen. I felt as though the foundation upon which I had built my identity, being gay, was crumbling. Over the subsequent weeks I read and prayed as I had failed to do for a very long time, with a fervour reminiscent of my first coming to Christ. You see, I had come to him again with the most difficult and painful aspects of my life. To learn again, that he had dealt with them through his death on the cross. To allow his grace and forgiveness to permeate my life and teach me that my identity and worth came from what he had accomplished. I was a forgiven sinner who was a beloved son of God the Father, and even Jesus himself was not ashamed to call me his brother.

I would not walk away from him again. I never saw the man I intended to be with, and I later heard he had found someone else. Sadly, I understand that he is now HIV positive.

I would love to tell you that my story has a perfect ending. It would be great to report that having turned away from my homosexual identity and practice, I have now married and had children. But that would be untrue. What is true is that my walk with Christ has deepened, and I feel secure in his mercy and love. Although I cannot change the past, I know I am not enslaved to it. Christ's death has brought a new beginning, and I am resolved to obey him in this, as in all other areas of my life. All that he has done and all that he will do is for my good and his greater glory, and I have his word on that! Praise him!

Emma

It all started around Easter three years back, when I realized that my life wasn't working very well. I had difficulties relating to my husband, my children, my family as well as my friends. I was having problems in my marriage and my children wore the brunt of my terrible mood swings. I was angry at my mother for not living up to my expectations of what a mother should be, and I was generally feeling unhappy with myself and life.

I started drinking heavily to numb the pain. This helped for a while, but it didn't fix the problems I had. I came to a point when I thought to myself, "What's the use? My life isn't worth living, nobody loves me, why should I continue this futile existence?"

I remember lying on my bed one night, crying, alone and severely cut off from everyone, thinking "There must be a way out. I don't want my life to be like this forever". The next morning I woke and decided to give an old friend of mine a call. She was a Christian and a child health nurse, and had been very supportive to me when my daughter was born. I went through postnatal depression and she had helped me get through that.

We met, and over lunch I told her how unhappy I was with my life. She told me about her walk with God and how he had changed her life. We started meeting together regularly to do a beginner's Bible study, and we became very close friends as we prayed and read the Bible together.

I was still experiencing a lot of problems with anxiety and depression, and I found myself becoming increasingly dependent on my friend. I idolized her and couldn't make any decision without first consulting her. If she wasn't "there for me" when I phoned, I would fall to pieces. I spent most of the day thinking about her, and I also started to have vivid sexual dreams about the two of us together. I thought I was in love with her.

I had actually experienced these feelings about several other women in the past, but had never acted on them. Thinking back to when I was at school, I always felt different from the other girls. I wasn't interested in boys, and I preferred to spend time with my father doing "guy stuff". My masculine side was overdeveloped and I was more into slot-cars, skateboards and sports than most of the boys I knew. I suppose going to an all-girls school didn't help. When I went through puberty I became aware of my sexual attraction towards certain girlfriends of mine.

Was I a lesbian? I didn't know for sure, but what I did know was that I was really confused, hurting, alone and very unhappy. I wanted someone to love me for who I was, so I resolved to tell my friend about the feelings I had towards her. Hopefully, she would feel the same way about me.

Her initial response was one of disbelief and withdrawal, and she said, "We should stop seeing each other for a while".

I was devastated. I had finally met someone whom I thought I could love and she rejected me! I wasn't going to take "no" for an answer, and so I kept phoning her. I became very manipulative, and I used every means at my disposal to win her over.

This went on for months, until one day we met for lunch again. She told me she had been speaking to some friends

about me, and they had given her the name of a Christian counsellor who might be able to help me. I thought I was using God
to get to her, but looking back I now know that God was using
her to get to me.

I realise now that this was an emotionally dependent relationship, and that I was looking to her to meet my needs rather
than looking to God to have them met. They were all legitimate
needs, caused by a lack of bonding with, and a defensive detachment from my mother. I had a same-sex love deficit and had
sexualized these needs into a lustful desire, and had tried to sat-
isfy them in my own way. These needs were to be met in
healthy, loving, non-sexual relationships with other women,
and God has certainly provided these women for me.

It was around this time that another good friend of mine
sensed that I was having some problems, and invited me to
come along to her church.

I remember the morning vividly. I woke up with a burning
desire to go to church! This was very strange for me, as I had come
from a non-Christian background. Shortly after this, my friend
asked me if I would like to join her Bible study group. I found the
leaders to be very encouraging, and well grounded in Christ. I
learnt a lot more about God's character from this home group, and
through these women I felt acceptance into God's family.

A really good relationship was formed between myself and
the leader of my home group. I felt I could trust her. She had
become a Christian at one of Billy Graham's crusades at the age
of thirteen. I told her about my problems, and she strongly recommended that I get some professional help—preferably from
a Christian counsellor.

I was initially reluctant to do this, but I can remember thinking, "OK, I'll give it a go, but I don't know how God can help me".

I was very apprehensive at my first meeting with the counsellor. I remember she told me, "Trust is the basis of any good relationship and it takes a while to build up this trust". As we continued with each session I started to feel more comfortable talking about myself, and we started to process events that had affected my attitudes to and perceptions of life.

I also found myself becoming increasingly drawn to God as I learnt more about his unconditional love and acceptance. Through counselling and prayer, God has revealed the roots of various forms of abuse, all of which needed to be dealt with and healed by him. I think that I actually stopped developing emotionally, to some degree, after these episodes. I became very introspective, stopped learning, and I believe there was a part of me that never really grew up. In a sense I was still a broken-hearted little girl, desperately in need of a big hug from Mum. I just wanted her to tell me everything would be okay and that she loved me.

A major breakthrough in my healing came when I asked God to forgive me for the anger and resentment I had held towards my mother for so many years. I also asked him to give me a new heart of love and compassion for those people who had hurt me in the past.

I was still having trouble understanding why I felt a sexual response to some women. My counsellor lent me a book on homosexuality entitled *Setting Love In Order* by Mario Bergner.[10] God really touched my heart while I was reading this book. It explained many of the reasons that contribute to a homosexual disposition, and gave great testimony to the healing power of Jesus in Bergner's life. Something which really struck me while reading this book was the fact that homosexuality or lesbianism is incompatible with what the Bible teaches about sexuality. I felt it was up to me to choose to either follow God and live my life by his standards, or to give in to my sin.

During a counselling session, while in prayer, I decided to make a commitment to Jesus and accept him as my Lord and Saviour. At that moment I knew God would be with me in my struggle from that day forward.

Another book I found most helpful was *Out Of Egypt* by Jeanette Howard. This is one of the best books I have read on lesbian-related issues. Howard speaks of her walk away from lesbianism, and the spiritual battle she encountered in making that choice. She gives great insights into what a person walking away from lesbianism will encounter, and how to get through these difficult times, as well as how to avail oneself of the help God offers. In the chapter on emotional dependency, she defines the term 'lesbian' as covering three categories of women.

First are those women who strive to fulfill sexual desires and emotional needs through other women. The second group have not acted out sexually, but have sought completion through an emotional relationship with another woman. The third category of lesbians are those who were too frightened to act upon their desires, so they resort to fantasy. Although one can engage in emotional dependency and never have a homosexual thought, emotional dependency frequently precedes lesbian sexual activity.[11]

Over the last three years, the counselling relationship I have been in has been a very important stage in my personal development and growth as a Christian. I have been on an incredible learning curve during this period, and I deeply value the gifts and insights of the people God has given to me on my journey.

The Liberty support group has also played a very important

part in my recovery. It was wonderful to know I wasn't the only Christian in the world who was struggling with unwanted homosexual feelings. Being able to share with these women and bring my deepest hurts before God in prayer with them has made a huge difference in my recovery. The teaching we received through the Sy Rogers videos has helped me to gain a greater understanding of the contributing factors behind a homosexual orientation, as well as how to deal with them.

The Liberty support group provided a safe and affirming environment where we could grow in our knowledge of Jesus, and learn to relate to each other in ways that were healthy. The praise and worship times were especially uplifting for me, and I still draw on those times and the songs we learnt when things get a bit bumpy. Seeing how God has worked in other peoples' lives was another huge encouragement. I felt a great affinity with the leaders, and found them all to be totally committed to this vital ministry. These leaders have also been a great example to me and I have learnt many valuable lessons from them.

I have now reached a place where I have experienced freedom from same-sex attraction and emotional dependency, things I have struggled with for over twenty-five years. This has only been possible through the people God has placed in my life. I believe that homosexuality and lesbianism are relational problems, and it is through relationships, both with Jesus and his people, that God administers his healing power.

My life has been blessed by God. My marriage is back on track, and I am growing more deeply in love with my husband every day. Our children are the great blessing of our union and we love them dearly.

I know I have not completed my healing process but I am well along the road to recovery. We are all on a journey, and with God's help we will get there.

Dazza

I had always believed in God, but did not do much more than believe. I went to Sunday School when I was young, and attended Scripture classes at infants and primary school, but never went to a regular church service. I used to watch a cartoon show on TV on Sunday mornings, and after the cartoon show finished a televangelism program called "Hour of Power" would begin. The "Hour of Power" was held at the Crystal Cathedral in California. The Cathedral is an impressive building, made of glass with gardens and fountains, and glass doors that open to a huge car park where people worship from their cars. I would watch the start of the program every week, then switch off after the first song to go surfing. One day I started to watch the whole program, and liked the gospel message that Jesus died to save me. I decided to attend my local Anglican church and get involved in it.

I became a Christian in my last year of school, when I was 18. I enjoyed my time at church, and became a youth group leader with the hope of meeting a lady youth group leader, getting married, and making our own youth group. However, there was a huge obstacle to this dream. I was gay.

Looking back, I could see why my homosexuality was going to develop. My father was an alcoholic who abused my mother and neglected the family. I never had a proper father/son relationship. When I was about eight or nine years old, I was sexually molested by a man who lived in the neighbourhood, and the molestation continued for a few years. After the molestation ceased I had strong desires for male sex. When I was thirteen, I commenced a gay relationship with a school friend who was a couple of years ahead of me. This relationship lasted for a few years, and ended when he moved from the area. The relationship had continued after I became a Christian. After it ended I did not see anyone for a few years. I knew that my homosexual actions were wrong, but I could not control my desires. I prayed that my desire would go away but it didn't. Masturbation on a daily basis became my release from sexual tension as I entertained my fantasies.

After a few years of not seeing anyone, I met a gay man and we became boyfriends in an on-again/off-again relationship over a period of ten years. Frequently on Friday nights after youth group we would get together, or we would get together on Saturday nights and I would leave on Sunday morning and go home to prepare for high school youth group that evening. I was entrenched in my homosexuality despite all my praying. I thought that I would change if I got married.

Due to circumstances at my local church, I decided to leave, and tried other churches. I visited a few, but none appealed to me. I stopped going to church but still remained a Christian. However I still struggled with my homosexuality, no matter how much I tried to resist it. It just didn't make sense. If I am gay then I can't be Christian. If I'm Christian then I can't be gay. There were days when I was fine being gay, and there were days when I loathed it. There were days when I felt like I was being ripped apart as I thought about the conflict of being gay and Christian. I would wake up in the morning with the sky blue, the sun shining brightly and the birds twittering. "It's going to be a beautiful day", I would think to myself and then the realization would hit me: "I'm still gay". Then I would drag myself out of bed and face the day as a gay man. The thought of waking up like this every day for the rest of my life was depressing. One day I was thinking of how overwhelmed I was by my troubles, and the thought of suicide entered my mind. I was shocked at myself for thinking this way, and about a month later I nearly drowned in a boating accident. The accident gave me a strong awareness of how precious life is and that I should appreciate it. As I lay in bed at the hospital, I couldn't help but think that this accident was from God, as if he was telling me, "Do you really want to have no life?".

A couple of months after the boating accident I went on holiday, and realized how lonely I was. I was not seeing my boyfriend at this time, and on my return from holiday I subscribed to a gay phone meeting service in the hope of finding "Mr Right". Prior to this I had visited a gay sex venue a few times in about 12 months, and I had for several years been going infrequently to a nude beach where the gay scene was prominent, in order to meet other men. I had many casual encounters, but nothing lasted for more than a few weeks as I was scared of being found out. One day, one of my best friends found out I was gay, and he told me that he was too. He had heard my message on the gay phone meeting service. It took me many months to get used to the idea that he knew, but eventually being gay became easier, knowing one of my best friends was also gay. We told each other our stories and would justify and affirm each other in our homosexuality.

I did not want to accept being gay, so I bought my first

book on the topic: *Homosexuality and the Politics of Truth* by Jeffrey Satinover.[12] It explained that homosexuality is changeable. I came out to a Christian friend. I had been his youth group leader for many years, and as he became older he and I would co-lead the groups. He did not condemn me, but showed sympathy for me. I told him how the confusion I felt was like being in the middle of a maze, not knowing which direction to go. I was also too scared to go in any direction. The book I was reading was giving me hope, but this hope was short lived—I recommenced seeing my boyfriend. Changing seemed impossible.

My gay best friend encouraged me to attend a gay mens' coming out group. He had been attending the group for several months, and he said it helped him to deal with his homosexuality. It was a drop-in emotional support group for gay men in the closet. They could attend and talk about the process of informing friends and family of their homosexuality, as well as learning about the different aspects of gay life. I used to think that I was the only Christian in the world struggling with homosexuality, but whilst attending the group I met other Christians who were gay. It made me feel better meeting the gay Christians, because I began to think that homosexuality and Christianity were compatible. However, there were many times at the group when I expressed my frustration at being gay, and my desire to be straight. The group would console me for the way I was feeling but could offer no real help. They would talk about how they came to terms with their homosexuality, saying "Once gay, always gay" and "You were born gay. Accept it".

I started to read books on pro-gay theology which were recommended to me by men in the group. *Stranger at the Gate* is an autobiography by Mel White,[13] in which he writes about his struggles as a gay man living in a Christian environment.

He eventually becomes a minister in a gay church. Bishop John Shelby Spong, a heterosexual Episcopalian in the USA, writes in his book, *Living in Sin?*[14] that homosexuality should be recognized within the church. Reading these books made me think that being gay and Christian could be compatible. At last I felt that after many years of struggling, I no longer needed to. I decided that I would go to the gay church, meet the man of my dreams, have a gay marriage and live gaily ever after.

It was a couple of weeks after I commenced going to the coming out group that a Christian friend, a mutual friend of my Christian friend whom I had come out to, asked me if I would like to attend his church. I had told him a few months earlier that I was not attending a church. After being out of church for 18 months, I started to attend another Anglican church. I would go to the coming out group on Sunday afternoons, then attend church after the group, and would continue 'husband-hunting' by attending gay venues and beats at other times of the week.

After I decided to accept my homosexuality in the understanding that it was compatible with Christianity, I rang up to find out the service times and meeting place of a gay church, but I never went to a service. I realized I did not want the watered-down pro-gay theology. I wanted the Truth, and I was more determined than ever to leave my homosexual past. I was no longer attached to anyone, as I had broken up with my boyfriend several months before, and the man I was seeing had gone overseas for a long period of time. I had the chance to break free from homosexuality, but after going down several pathways of the maze that I was in, I found that I was back in the middle of the maze again, and unsure of how to go about leaving homosexuality.

I went to my friend who had invited me to his church, and

told him that I did not want to be gay, and that I had thought of attending the gay church but I no longer wanted watered-down pro-gay theology. I told him I wanted the Truth. I told him how lost and confused I was, and that I did not know what to do about my problem. He had been to a Christian men's conference earlier in the year, where the gay issue was brought up. He was able to get me the phone number of an organization which could help. He, like my other friend, didn't condemn me, but offered support, encouragement and prayers. He gave me the phone number for Liberty Christian Ministries. I spoke to someone from Liberty and they told me their story. I was told about the support groups and the need to see a counsellor, and it was recommended I read *Desires in Conflict* by Joe Dallas.[15] I went along to a church to hear a talk by Liberty. After having contact with Christians, gays, and gay Christians, this was the first time I realized that there were ex-gay Christians.

I commenced counselling and attending the Liberty support group eleven months ago. The Liberty support group has been extremely helpful, and I have nearly completed my second group. The video tapes by Sy Rogers have been good as I have been able to learn so much about myself and why I became gay. Things started to make sense as I realized that I was having my same-sex needs met in an improper way, and learned how to have my same-sex needs met in a wholesome way. Receiving and giving support from the small group is helpful. We can talk openly and candidly about the issues that are confronting us, without feeling condemned. Talking about my personal life has been hard, but relating to the other members has allowed me to develop trust in people, which is something that I could not do previously.

Counselling sessions have been painful. It has not been easy to talk about my past, and of the shame I felt for being molested, as I blamed myself for the molestation. There have been many times at counselling when I have broken down and cried, and in between sessions I have cried myself to sleep as I worked through the hurts and pain of my past. Counselling has also been joyful. Dealing with the different aspects of my past has allowed me to be released from shame and guilt, and much healing has taken place.

A couple of gay friends were concerned for my mental well-being when I informed them of my decision to leave homosexuality. There has been much conflict between myself and them about homosexuality and its incompatibility with Christianity. At one stage there were weekly confrontations. These gay men were people I knew socially, and I still wanted to be friends with them, as being gay was not the common aspect of our friendship. The conflict increased when Liberty was slandered in the gay press when they had to cancel their annual conference because of threats from gay militants. I went into damage control as I defended myself, the work of Liberty and Christianity. I put up with much criticism as my gay friends thought I was going to turn into a homophobe. It was a battle to make them realise that the articles about Liberty were full of lies. It made me realise that I needed much more support. I looked at the congregation of the evening service at my church and thought, "they are part of God's mighty army and I need their support". I told my story to my minister, who was very supportive, and told him what I wanted to do. He gave me the opportunity to give my testimony. There were about 50 people at the service when I did so. Not one of them rejected me, and I received much affirmation on the night. For me it was a relief to tell them about myself, as opposed to them finding out from other people. My disclosure has helped me become closer to a good number of people. This closeness, trust and honesty in relating to both sexes has been very therapeutic. When there are times that I feel down because of my homosexuality, it is good to be able to tell my fellow Christians and home bible study group so I can be prayed for. My congregation have shown me so much love and respect. I cannot thank God enough for the blessing of these wonderful Christians whom he has placed in my life.

My homosexuality has greatly diminished in the first eleven months, but I am still in the recovery process and may be so for many more years. Although change cannot happen fast enough, I must learn to be patient. One of the memory verses I learnt when I became a Christian is Isaiah 40:31: "Those who hope in the Lord will renew their strength. They will soar on wings like eagles, they will run and not grow weary, they will walk and not be faint".

I do not know what my future will be, but I look forward to it as I continue to trust in God. Today I am a more positive person, as I am no longer shackled by sexual sin. My relationship with my family, especially my father, has greatly improved. I do look forward to getting married and starting the youth group, but I know that I can be happy in life as a single man too as I maintain a right relationship with God and right relationships with people.

Robin

I have now been out of the gay lifestyle for seven years; and although I am not completely 'healed', I am well on the way.

My journey away from homosexuality, and towards healing, started one night after a sports presentation. We had won the Grand Final, and I had won the award for the "best and fairest" player for the fourth time in succession. I was quite drunk, not because I was happy, but because I felt empty and depressed. I had reached what I considered at that time to be the top; but instead of feeling excited and proud, I was miserable. Instead of being pleased for me, my friends were jealous. I felt everything was meaningless and empty.

I had been in and out of many sexual relationships with both men and women, and was totally confused about my sexuality. I knew somewhere deep inside that I didn't want a gay relationship, but it filled my overwhelming emotional need for affection and nurturing that I had never had from my mother as a child. I was living a double life: an angel during the week when I was at home with my parents, and at the weekend erupting out of my closet into my lesbian lifestyle.

As I drove home that night, my loneliness almost over-

57

whelmed me. There had to be something more. I was so low, I tried to run my car off the road and end it all. Fortunately for me I missed the pole I was aiming at, and I just sat in the middle of the road and cried my heart out.

I knew I needed help because I was bottled up emotionally, but I felt I couldn't talk to anyone about my confused feelings. If I had spoken to my gay friends they would have encouraged me to accept the 'gay way'. I didn't feel able to talk to anyone else for fear they wouldn't understand, and I thought they wouldn't accept or help me anyway.

Finally this isolation was broken when I was able to confide in a Christian woman I met. It took time, but I was able to respond to the love of Jesus I saw in this friend. I was open to this as I had come from a Catholic background, and already had an awareness of God. I then started to attend the same church as my friend, and eventually became linked in with that congregation.

At this time I moved out of a live-in lesbian relationship and also away from many of my gay friends. I found it hard to trust most people in the church, so it was a very lonely time.

I heard about a Christian recovery programme which was being run for people who were wanting to deal with homosexuality. I was accepted into the course. This was the breakthrough I needed. The programme ran for almost a year, and during this time my faith began to grow as I saw my life and the lives of others in the group being healed. As I began to trust the love of those around me, I was enabled to trust God's love in a deeper way. I was encouraged and moved that these people genuinely wanted to help me, as I thought of myself as a terrible sinner. For the first time I experienced unconditional love, and I could hardly believe that they didn't want anything in return. The couple leading the group provided me with a valuable and healthy parental role model and a structure of love and discipline, as well as showing me what a good Christian marriage could be like.

It was also a time of great pain and many tears as God took me through his process of healing. At times I was frightened by the changes that were happening to me, and there were times when I was tempted to go back to my former friends. None of this was easy. It was a little like climbing out of a canyon. But once I was on my way it eventually became easier to keep going, rather than to stop and go back to the cycle of hopelessness I had felt. Some nights I was so lonely I would just cry out to God to comfort me—and each time I would feel his presence with me, giving me the comfort I so desperately needed.

The important question for me, and the one I continually asked God, was, "How could this love which seems so right be so wrong?". My answer came from Romans 1:24-25, and it made sense to me. I had exchanged the truth about God's love for an imitation, and worshipped and served the created things rather than him. I could see I had done this to meet my overwhelming need for the legitimate love I had never received. But I could also see that it hadn't worked.

The other thing that brought deep healing for me was being able to forgive my father. I had seen him as overbearing, rejecting and uninterested in his children. He was such a negative influence in my life that I saw him as being responsible for destroying hope in me. He was incapable of encouraging any of us, and because of his attitude I felt cheated of my happiness as a child. Being able to forgive him has brought understanding and tolerance on my part. He has improved in his relating to me, and as a result of forgiving him, I can now respond (rather than react) to him. We still have a way to go, but we are getting there.

My life has changed for the better. I can now feel a sense of belonging and identity that comes from being secure in God. He has met me in my loneliness, and he is providing me with the healthy, loving relationships I need.

Mother

Sarah

A little over three years ago, my son called my husband and me together, asked us to sit down, and told us that he should have been born a girl and was taking steps to become female.

His story was one of great pain from his earliest memories.

In the infants' class at school, he felt that he should have been playing with girls, but was sent to play in the boys' playground. He was very much a loner, made few friends, and did not join in any sport willingly.

During his early teens, he said that he had tried to communicate his confusion to his father and to me on different occasions, but had never managed to get the words out.

In his final year at school, he began a relationship with a girl two years his junior. Although it seemed at times to be very strained, it continued, and he married her when he was 32. The marriage lasted 12 years, during which time he fathered a child, and apparently cross-dressed on occasions. Though we knew nothing of this at that time, it was obvious that the marriage was far from ideal. When he announced that he and his wife were going to have a 'trial separation' for a few months, the announcement came as no surprise.

It seems that he had sought help, began some hormone therapy, and the die was cast.

My immediate reaction was one of disbelief. This was followed by fervent prayer that God would deliver my son from deception, would restore him to his right mind, would heal him, and anything else I could think of. My mind was totally closed to the possibility that he would continue with his desire to live as a woman.

My husband's reaction, on the other hand, was one of shock; but he also had a determination to try to understand what the problem was, and to relate to William (as I will call him) as openly as possible. He read every book that he could on the subject (not many books were available, he found), and tried to discuss the matter with William. However, the distress caused showed itself in a new cancer developing (he had had a previous cancer and had been in remission for some time), and within months he was back in hospital. In August he died, seven months after William's disclosure.

The day after the funeral, William presented himself to the world dressed as a female, and has remained so ever since.

I did have a choice not to see him. And in one way, on reflection, that would have been the easier option. It seems that most parents of transsexuals do that. Some of my family couldn't meet him, but for me it was not an option.

I couldn't handle seeing him in female attire so soon after my husband's death, for which I felt, at that stage, that he was responsible. But we did communicate by phone regularly. Finally, in the following January I invited him to come to lunch.

Never will I forget that day. He knocked on the door and stood just outside my line of sight, so that I had to actually open the door before I saw him. He was dressed tidily in jeans and a t-shirt, but with women's low-heeled shoes—and a wig. A long one.

One of the sad things that had happened during his later teen years was that he began to lose his hair. By this time he had only a fringe of hair around the back of his head and over his ears. He had let this grow very long of late, and it had looked most untidy. But now it was all covered by a wig. As I bent forward to kiss him, my mouth met the wig, which just about finished me. However, we managed to get beyond that and sat down to lunch. I discovered that he also was wearing make up—not very expertly applied.

Over the next weeks I struggled to relate to him. I found it was better to speak openly about difficulties I encountered en route—for instance, I still called him William, because my mouth kept stumbling over his chosen female name (which I will give as Marina). I told him about that, and he responded positively, knowing that I was seeking to be as positive as I could and trying to accept who he was or who he thought he was.

Again, after I found that I was reacting negatively to misapplied lipstick, I had a word with him about how to put it on. I felt quite sick doing this, but his response was so appreciative that I was glad I had managed to.

Then in December he underwent surgery to remove his genitals. Medical people told me that there is a high suicide rate afterwards—about 80% of people attempt it because they find that the operation hasn't fulfilled their expectations, and they are not suddenly content and complete as they had anticipated.

The only thing I could think of taking to the hospital was a Bible—a pocket one I had, to put in his drawer. He did appreciate it and said he'd like to keep it.

In the meantime, I had contacted two friends who I knew had been in ministry to homosexuals. They were then with Liberty Christian Ministries, and amongst other things were running a support group for parents, family and friends of peo-

WHAT SOME OF YOU WERE

ple in that lifestyle. We understood that transsexuality is not at all the same as homosexuality, but I was eager for any help and found great comfort in the support I found there. Although others in the group could not identify with me, at least they could grieve with me and pray and love me, as I did for them in their areas of distress.

And so we worked through the second year. And I discovered a lot of things.

I discovered another mother in a similar situation—the only one I could find—and she lived in Singapore, so I went to see her and talk and pray the situation through.

I discovered that transsexuality is not caused by a desire to express oneself as the opposite sex in sexual activity. In fact it seems to have very little, if anything, to do with sexual activity. It has to do with identity. It is about who he or she feels she/he is, at the very heart of their being. It is an orientation, not a sexual urge or need.

I discovered that I did not feel guilty in any way. Since I had not been conscious of his struggle during those growing up years, I had nothing to reproach myself with.

I discovered that in spite of my own difficulty in responding to him in a natural way, he was still my offspring and I was still his mother. And God and I both loved him.

And I discovered that God is bigger than the problem.

I don't know how it will all end. I do know that he/she (I still stumble) is quite ego-centric, and that this is part of the problem. I do know that the child of the marriage has suffered, but that God is bringing him through it in some quite amazing ways. I do know that family bonds are strengthened greatly, and I do know that God is in charge.

A few months ago I was being prayed for at a conference (about something else) when the Lord said to me, "I want you to give me the two deaths". The first was that of my husband, of course, but it hadn't occurred to me until then that for me, my son had died. I did manage to give them to him, and I know he's continuing to take me and others on this strange journey, and that a lot of things I used to be quite certain of, I am now not so sure about.

There's only one thing in this world I can be sure of, and that's the Cross. I know that when Jesus died he took this grief of both my son/daughter and myself. I know that he is the Healer and that healing will come, probably in ways that I don't expect, as I choose to keep focussed on him, get on with the journey he has called me on, and meet the continuing challenges in his strength, not in mine.

And I know that as I continue to walk and learn, God gets bigger and bigger.

The story of Jane: a mother's perspective

Two years ago, when I initially began to write this story, I was not able to. My emotional state prevented me from doing so. But through the grace, love and faithfulness of God, I can now write an account of my experience of being the mother of a homosexual daughter.

Initially, in my distress and confusion, I asked God "Why?". A friend once said to me, "God doesn't make mistakes". I am now in a position to acknowledge that what has happened is part of God's plan for our family. I believe and cling to God's promise in Jeremiah 29:11:

> "For I know the plans I have for you", declares the Lord, "plans to prosper you and not to harm you, plans to give you hope and a future".

In recording this story, it was difficult to know where to start. After much reflection and soul searching, I decided to start with my wedding day.

This marriage brought together two young (20 and 21 year old) adults, who came from very different upbringings. John's family were not close. He was left without a father as a teenager, and he grew up with a passion for sport. He had never attended church.

Home life for my family was important, and I became a conscientious school student and enjoyed indoor activities. My siblings and I were sent to Sunday School and also attended church regularly. I could have been described as a person who was trying to live by "good deeds", never having a personal relationship with God.

John and I both wanted our family life to be happier than it was in the homes we left behind.

After ten years of marriage, we were blessed with two daughters. Three years later, I was expecting my third child. I remember wondering at the time how I would cope with this latest addition to our family. My husband was working long hours in our business, and was unable to provide a great deal of support in looking after our girls. We had no family support.

As a result of my medical history, Jane was born by caesarean section.

I did not breastfeed her because of past failure and the constraints of time. I had to drive children to school and pre-school, carry out household chores, and help John in our business. We loved all three of our daughters and worked hard to give them everything we could. We tried to encourage their talents. As the children grew up, their differences were apparent. Our first two daughters, like me, enjoyed indoor activities. From an early age, Jane loved to play outdoors.

When the older girls were at school, Jane and I experienced much frustration. She wanted me to play outdoors with her (there were no other young children living in our neighbourhood), and I wanted to get on with household tasks. Since we had by now sold our business, I took a part-time job to pay for Jane to attend pre-school, in the belief that it would provide the opportunities she needed for outdoor play and socialization with children of her own age.

Relatives and friends often made comments about Jane being a 'tomboy' and the 'boy' her father never had. Her preference for clothing became apparent. She refused to wear dresses, wanting only to wear pants. It was difficult to buy anything for her that she would wear. Jane also seemed to crave attention. Once, when one of our other daughters had something important happening in her life, Jane was 'sick', which ensured that our attention was focussed on her. We can recall other attention-seeking incidents. As a young child, Jane developed a worrying habit. It started with her touching her genitals, and later she began to masturbate regularly. We sought professional help for this, and met with a range of responses from "There is no need to worry as long as she does it in the privacy of her bedroom", to actual outrage that we would suggest a young child would do such a thing.

Each of our children was encouraged to participate in sporting activities, but Jane excelled in all sports and my husband John was keen to develop her talents. This caused many arguments between John and me, which frequently involved Jane. John believed in the necessity for Jane to train and participate daily in sporting activities. I was concerned about her school work, the fact that she was not attending Sunday school and that our family life was suffering since John was also involved with training and the administration of our children's sport.

Jane loved her sporting lifestyle, and was anxious to please her Dad by performing well. She was selected for many representative sporting teams, both for school and open ladies' competitions, and was often the youngest team member. This involved many trips away within NSW and interstate. Men's teams often travelled with the girls. On several occasions when Jane was touring, she witnessed inappropriate sexual behaviour between team members.

In her later teens, I was concerned about an attachment Jane had to a female school friend. John and I disagreed about the time they were spending together. This developed into an emotionally dependent relationship for her. Once again, our family life was adversely affected. In particular, my relationship with my daughter was affected, since Jane felt that I was opposed to her friendship. The relationship with her friend eventually developed into a sexual one. When the friendship broke up, Jane was devastated, and eventually revealed her true problem—her struggle with homosexuality.

Years of turmoil followed for Jane, John and myself. Thankfully she and I had many conversations, which helped me to put together the pieces of the puzzle of the problem I was facing. I now recognize God's hand in the situation also.

I had not attended church for some years. Just before Jane had disclosed her homosexuality, I had been thinking about how a marriage which had started out with such hope could go so wrong, and our family life disintegrate so badly. God, in his grace, was preparing me for what was to come, giving me the revelation that I should once more attend church. On the first visit, I indicated my desire to dedicate my life, and publicly accepted Christ as my Saviour some twelve months later.

Meanwhile, I felt the need to find out all about homosexuality, what causes it and what could be done to help my daughter.

I read extensively about the topic, attended a seminar presented by Sy Rogers (a man who teaches on the subject of homosexuality from a Christian perspective) and a parents' support group at Liberty. I am particularly grateful to the Liberty staff, who were largely instrumental in helping me to gain a healthy perspective on the situation.

Jane initially sought help from people in a local church, who introduced her to a recovering lesbian. This person became a close friend to Jane, and thankfully helped her through years of struggle with the feelings. At her friend's urging, Jane left home and went to live with a group of young people. I still question the need for her to have done this, but we were supportive of her decision. Still struggling, Jane attended Cornerstone, a Christian community in country NSW where God's word is studied. After staying for six months, she returned home and was baptized as a Christian at the church she was attending. She also had people pray over her in an attempt to be free of her homosexual feelings. Jane formed a relationship with a young man but that lasted only a short time.

After attending a support group for Christians wishing to deal with their unwanted same-sex attractions, and extensive counselling, Jane made the decision to live as a lesbian. To this day she is living in a relationship with her partner Julie.

The following is a summary of what I believe contributed, in some ways, to my daughter's homosexuality:

Jane was able to sense the stress I was feeling even before she was born.

The timing of her birth was at the convenience of a doctor who was soon to depart for overseas.

Although she was always nursed when she was fed, Jane was not breastfed, and could have missed out on the close bonding which comes from breastfeeding.

At the age of three, Jane and her older sister were sent to my mother's home in the country for six weeks whilst I recovered from major surgery. I had further surgery eighteen months later.

Jane is a very sensitive person, easily hurt, and craves affirmation and demonstrative love. We were not overtly demonstrative in our love, but indicated it in more practical ways. Jane misunderstood this as lack of care and concern for her.

Anti-social behaviour developed from what I now believe was anxiety brought about by her feelings of insecurity and inadequacy. We possibly failed to handle this problem sensitively, which added to her anxiety.

There were misunderstandings—did I take the time to explain to her why she was going to pre-school? Did she know that I loved her at this time? Did she see this as rejection? Jane's response was to 'shut down' emotionally from me to prevent being hurt. She distinctly remembers the incident. From this time I believe she was unable to receive any love that I offered.

Jane perceived a difference between herself and her sisters, and felt some confusion about it.

Jane internalized the names she was called ('tomboy'), and began to act out the behaviour she thought was expected of her.

John and I failed to relate properly. Unkind words were spoken, and frustration was expressed angrily and inappropriately. Jane felt personally responsible for our arguments, since many of them involved issues relating to her.

We failed to affirm her femininity—Jane was encouraged to be an aggressive sportswoman.

Jane was affected by the promiscuous behaviour of others, and to some extent her perception from her home life that women and their work were not as important as men in our society.

Her feelings of being unloved led to forming a co-dependent relationship.

She finally made the decision that she is homosexual and will live her life that way.

After working through this situation I am now able to say thanks to God, for he certainly got my attention. I can now pray with a grateful heart from Psalm 119:71: "It was good for me to be afflicted so that I might learn your decrees".

I have taken responsibility for my failures in nurturing my daughter. I take comfort in knowing that God is the judge of each one of us, and he knows all the aspects of the story. I know that God has forgiven me, and I believe in Psalm 103:12 "As far as the east is from the west, so far has he removed our transgressions from us".

My role now is to pray faithfully for Jane. I am praying that God will help me to love her and her partner unconditionally, and show me how to do that. (Jane has been interstate for some time and is planning to return soon.) I pray for strength and guidance to go on with my own life. I have learned that God is faithful, and while I have the support of some very good friends, I am now putting all my trust and hope in God. Proverbs 3:5-6 tells me to "Trust in the Lord with all your heart and lean not on your own understanding; in all your ways acknowledge him, and he will make your paths straight".

76

Daughter

78

Audrey

/ was 19 when I found out that my father was a homosexual. I was shocked and disillusioned, but also I felt that this made sense of the strange parent he had been. My mother died when I was six. The care of raising my brother (who was two years older than I) and me fell upon my grandmother who was 76. Dad's excessive drinking was punctuated with violent outbursts, and this behaviour resulted in a very strained atmosphere at home. We were always relieved when he didn't come home. Strangely enough (to us), he had numerous friendships with much younger men whom he brought home on weekends.

He disliked my faithful old grandmother, and when I reached puberty he also turned with a fury upon my blossoming expression of womanhood. Soon he became obsessed with the fact that I was immersed in the wild 70's world of sex and drugs—neither of which I was very interested in or successful at. Simultaneously, his obsession with my brother grew. So when I learned of his sexual orientation, I suppose I felt I understood something of his behaviour.

I left home at 17 and travelled overseas, becoming a Christian, and eventually marrying and having two children.

Dad was a severe alcoholic at this stage. When I returned to Australia, his life seemed to be a living anguish. He reached out to Jesus as I talked to him about my faith, and he became a Christian. His conversion was genuine, but at this stage he was well known amongst young male prostitutes, who frequented his house and called him whenever they needed to earn some money. He never discussed his homosexuality with me, and in fact that was one word I happily omitted from the English language whenever we were together.

Dad joined a large Pentecostal church in the early 80's, but even though he was such a needy man he was unable to be honest with anyone about his problems. His young fellowship leader and his wife, I'm sure, felt totally inadequate to deal with him, and there were no groups such as Liberty in existence at that time to support him.

Ultimately Dad backslid, and began cohabiting with a young man five years younger than myself. This relationship bought some stability to his life. My children didn't know about his sexual orientation at that time as they were too small.

I suppose I wasn't actually too anxious about Dad having contact with my children. His homosexuality was exclusively with young men about 18 years of age or thereabouts, whom I'm sure reminded him of my brother. He was very fond of young children, but I felt quite confident in my understanding of his sexuality that it wasn't a risk to my children. His partner was generally at work during the week, so our paths only crossed at weekends. He was a lovely, gentle, sincere guy, around whom I also felt my children were quite safe. Of course, I would never have let them spend a night at their grandfather's, but we included Dad and his lover quite a lot in our lives. When my daughter and son were old enough to cope, I told them about their grandfather. I wanted them to hear it from me before they heard it from anyone else.

My father died when I had just turned 32.

I regret that Dad couldn't have been more open with me. I gather his homosexuality was founded in sexual abuse by a wealthy neighbour. This, coupled with Dad's abject poverty in his childhood, had a profound influence on his life. I've pieced these snippets of information together from one of Dad's friends, who was also gay but became a Christian around the same time as Dad. It has helped me enormously in my understanding of my father, as well as the causes of his homosexuality.

I don't know how I would have handled the situation had the children been older and more aware. Maybe I would have reassessed the situation as my son reached the desirable age of youth favoured by Dad.

I remember being hysterical when AIDS was first discovered, and nobody quite knew how it was transmitted. I was so concerned for the children. I was in my bedroom praying, and I felt the overwhelming presence of God fill me and assure me that they would never contract the disease. I carried that assurance in my heart and never worried about it after that. Dad was also an active carrier of Hepatitis B, which I used to worry about because he'd take bites out of the children's food and then return it to their plates

My husband's attitude to Dad was horrible. Even though Dad's behaviour was much too intrusive into our lives, instead of outright confrontation, or better still moving us to another region

geographically isolated from him, my husband let resentments just fester away. He also judged Dad's sexual bondage in a loveless, silent, yet condemnatory fashion. Dad used to bring his young male prostitute friends over to our home pretending they were drug addicts he was counselling. That was another guise he used to access young men: he worked as a drug counsellor.

As for me—I have faced life with perhaps very little personal infrastructure. I once went to see a wise Anglican minister during a period of backsliding. I was amazed how most people could lead normal productive lives without Jesus, yet whenever I tried to leave Jesus out of my life I was wiped out. When I questioned him about this, his answer was profound. He said that most children are raised in homes where precepts and foundations of love, respect, lawfulness, honesty, peace and dignity are laid down to be built upon later. He also said that not only were these not laid down for me, but quite the converse had happened—lying, stealing, cheating, abuse, aggression, violence and so on were established instead. Without Jesus to guide, heal and nurture me I can't survive.

On many occasions I've felt the compassion and intervention of Jesus in my life. At critical moments he has truly met even my primal needs. I need to walk closely with him and to be dependent upon him—but perhaps this is in fact a blessing. I know without him I'm nothing, so the trap of dependence upon myself and not God is one I can't endure for long, even if I fall into it.

Wife

Laura

The revelation

Two and a half years ago was a huge turning point in my marriage of fifteen years. In less than a week, a death occurred in the family; a court case was pending; and my husband revealed to me the shocking secrets of his life—his involvement, for many years during and before our marriage, in homosexuality.

Numbness

I was all alone. I felt numb, grief stricken, sad, angry, and I did not know where to go from here.

No-one knew except our minister. My husband had confided in him just two days after telling me. Our minister spent some time with me and prayed with me. I knew he cared, but he was new to the church and therefore hadn't known us well.

I didn't want help. I was scared. I felt humiliated. I didn't want others to know about this situation. I knew it wasn't my fault, but who wants your friends to know that not only has your husband been unfaithful, but with other men at that?

In a strange way, I also felt tied up in this awful mess—this included financial problems as well, as he had recently lost his employment. God was there—I knew that. I prayed and cried to him that first night as I lay alone in my bed. The Psalms were some comfort at this time. One of my early questions was: "Lord, you brought us together in a Christian marriage. Why did you lead me into this marriage, to have children, with this as the outcome?"

Help

One of the first things I said to my husband was, "Whatever happens to us in the future, one thing I know you need, is help and counselling". He agreed—he knew this, and had wanted help in the past but didn't know where to find it.

His secret was out and he was relieved. Its hold on him was, to a large extent, broken. As I later read, involvement with homosexuality was like an addiction—the more secret it was, the greater its lure.

In the ensuring two to three months, when our children were in bed or away, we sat in the evening and talked. He had revealed the basics of his life in those first few days, but still had much to tell me. I needed to know—it was like opening an old musty cupboard and dispelling the ugly ghosts within. It was painful for both of us, but needed to be done. He was extremely exhausted after our sessions. He was now in part-time work, which was God's provision as it gave time for counselling, talking and sorting out some pressing problems.

Before this revelation, I knew a little about Sy Rogers and his ministry through friends who had heard him at a conference in Sydney. They had been very impressed with his work and testimony, and bought his video. My friend had lent me this tape. That fateful week I pulled it out to watch it. We both watched it separately. I found it very informative and encouraging. I could see how God worked in the nitty gritty.

I think this is when I heard of Liberty Christian Ministries as well. Our minister had also heard of Liberty, and encouraged us to contact them. He also helped us find a good Christian psychologist to see. We subsequently saw him separately and together for many months. Some people in our church lovingly gave financially for my counselling.

A church worker/friend spoke to me ten days after my shocking news. She had been given the bare bones of my predicament. I struggled with her having this knowledge. "Can we meet sometime?" she asked.

"Can you cope with hearing what I know?" I asked, trying to fight back the tears. Could our friendship be the same, I wondered? Could she face my husband again, having this information? I knew that once we met I would need to confide in her, and didn't know if we could both cope with that. God's love and power is bigger than my small brain!

Through prayer and sharing over many weeks I received much help and strength to face my problems. We contacted Liberty. My husband spent time on the phone with them, but eventually joined a support group similar to Liberty that was in our area.

I was invited to a Liberty support group for spouses and parents of those struggling with homosexuality. I was also put in touch with another wife who had some similar experiences. At that time, the group met monthly, and I went regularly for two years until it disbanded. There is still contact between some of us. The wonderful thing about this group was its acceptance of each other, and the prayer support. Apart from feeling loved and free to share my sorrows, I laughed and cried with others about their loved ones. It was also informative as we watched tapes and discussed various issues. Through this group, and meeting regularly with my friend at church, I learnt to bring joys and sorrows before God in prayer. We saw many answers. The support group showed me others' needs—I was not alone.

Some parents felt so frustrated and unable to share with friends at church. "How did it happen, where did we go wrong?" they asked themselves. Our group met for us. We needed time out. We could be honest and know that what was said would go no further.

More help

There came a time when we had to tell our son and daughter something of their father's past. They were in their early teens. I honestly don't know what this has meant to them. However, we are functioning fairly well as a family, and their lives at this stage are very normal.

Some months later we had a huge hurdle to face. By now a number of people had been informed. Support was great. A few found the news very difficult; some needed time. Liberty spoke at our church, and the response was very encouraging. Through this latest ordeal, prayer support was strong—a small group prayed with us the night before. We came through this. I learnt to rely on God more deeply as my own fears and anxieties would try to take over. Matthew 11:28-29 is great! "Come to me, all you who are weary and burdened, and I will give you rest. Take my yoke upon you and learn from me, for I am gentle and humble in heart, and you will find rest for your souls." That promise calmed my mind. Resting in him—wonderful, comforting, refreshing.

One friend who sensed I had needs but didn't know what, discovered the news. She chided herself that she hadn't come to me earlier. I assured her that I probably couldn't have told her anyway. Now that she knew, it was a relief. Consequently a small group of women started meeting with me regularly for prayer. Here was another place I could be open and share particular needs and concerns. Three of us still continue to meet for prayer; however, we now pray for all of us and our families. Although this group has now broadened in its aims, it continues to be a place where I can share particular concerns and answers to prayer regarding homosexual issues.

Now, two and a half years down the track, my husband and I are still together. We have our ups and downs. We have worked through a lot of issues. I have had to learn to trust him again, as he has been able to be honest with me, and come to terms with his struggles and deal with issues in his past.

Accountability has been important for me. My husband endeavours to keep me informed about himself. He rings me if he is going to be late home, or is held up in traffic. If he is having a tough time in his personal life, he also tries to let me know. Knowledge is empowering. I have found it better to know the worst and deal with it, than to be ignorant. Sometimes there are misunderstandings, or he is held up at work, and I panic. I know I need to trust God in these times of fear.

Where do we fit in? I struggle with this question. I often feel uncomfortable with other couples who do not know about my husband. Some of our close friends know in part the road he has travelled, and how God has dealt with him and provided for us. Some people, perhaps, are still back at the beginning, trying to make sense of the whole homosexual issue, while others are ignorant of our tale. I don't know how to relate to all these people, but as my friend once advised: "we all have sin in our lives that God has to deal with—we do not need to know about the dark side of everyone's life".

Another issue is how faithful God has been, and how he has strengthened both of us. I am unable to share these good things with those who do not already know my story; just as I am unable to share the past.

The future

The future has some unknowns. Some of the past may catch up with him. I have no control over this, and he cannot change what has happened. Sometimes I grieve for the past, and grieve for the good things in our married past that have been tainted with the ghosts of his homosexual life. In my darker moments, I yearn for more Christian men to be proactive in being prayerfully supportive with my husband, as others have been with me. I have some unanswered questions. But I am certain that my life is in God's hands and that our future is also hopeful.

Recently my husband and I attended a Liberty prayer night. We both found it tremendously encouraging. He met somebody who asked him why he was there. He told her why and what his past had been. That's good news! God is good. This was the first time he had been able to tell somebody he didn't know, outside of his support group, someone who could have assumed he was there only for the needs of others.

The Psalmist's prayer helped me a lot in those early days:

> Though you have made me see troubles many and bitter, you will restore my life again, from the depths of the earth you will again bring me up. You will increase my honour and comfort me once again (Psalm 71:20-21).

90

Sara

*H*aving been married for less than a year, I made the shocking discovery that my husband was having sex with men.

This led to a big confrontation, in which I was accused of being the cause of his infidelity. I agreed to set about trying to 'fix' the marriage. It didn't take me very long to realise that I couldn't 'fix' the marriage. I also realized that I wasn't the cause of his homosexuality. That had started a long time before I met him. I knew before we were married that he had been actively involved in the 'gay' lifestyle for 20 years. I married him in spite of that because, since he was a Christian, I thought that he was healed. Of course, later on I realized how totally naive this was. I thought I would be the one who would love him more than anyone else had ever been able to, and I would be the one to fill the void in his life.

As his promiscuous behaviour continued, I realized that I could not continue in the marriage as it was. I left. The only safe place for me to go was back home to live with my parents where I found the love and support I needed at the time. Leaving the marriage was, perhaps, the start of the process of recovery for me. I was in shock and denial for about six months. I thought I

91

was in a nightmare which I hoped would be over soon. I felt a failure, as I had expected my Christian marriage to be a lasting one. In some weird way I also felt responsible for the break-up. I felt betrayed, confused, isolated and helpless.

I was desperate to talk to someone who could relate to my experience, ideally someone who had been through a similar experience. I didn't find anyone. It also would have been helpful if there had been some sort of support group available for spouses—there wasn't. I finally went to a couple who worked with Christians who wanted to deal with their homosexuality. This couple listened to me, and gave me some helpful insights and were supportive. I am so grateful for the support I received from them.

One of the practical suggestions they made was to be tested for sexually transmitted diseases. They referred me to a Christian GP who was sensitive and understanding. Even though this had been handled in a very caring way, just needing to have these very necessary tests left me feeling dirty and cheap, and it was a most humiliating experience. It all added to my sense of betrayal. I had not asked for any of it, and here I was being tested for HIV, Hepatitis B, chlamydia and the rest— all of which, thankfully, were negative.

I needed to understand about homosexuality, and what had driven my husband in that area. I was greatly helped by participating in a programme that this same couple ran. It went for about a year, and during the course of that group I gained many insights into the roots of homosexuality.

The group consisted of both men and women. As I interacted with them, I not only grew in my understanding of their struggles, but I also received love and care and felt understood. It also caused me to look at many of my own issues, which included family and sexuality issues. It was a group where I felt safe to discuss these areas of my life. It was a group where I had to relate to both lesbians and homosexual men, so I had to deal with my own prejudices, some of which I didn't even know I had!

Also helpful at this time were certain friendships. Some friends couldn't cope with what had happened, and were silent or absent, while others were truly supportive. They listened, took me out, invited me in for meals, sent letters and just generally loved me. This built me up and restored my dignity and self worth.

The most unhelpful thing was the lack of support and understanding I received from the church. The minister didn't want to know, and abdicated his responsibility totally. Even though he knew my husband had been a practising homosexual, he didn't raise the issue before we were married, and after the marriage broke up he was unable to support either of us. The church leaders didn't want to know, either. They were ill-equipped emotionally and practically to handle the situation, and many of the people in the church were just ignorant. I suppose the last straw for me was when I was told by a senior lady in the church that "what God had joined together I must not separate".

I left that church.

I wish I had been able to speak up for myself more at this time, but I couldn't. It's taken a number of self-help groups, and hours of counselling, to even be able to talk about it without falling apart. My reason for telling this story is to let the church know that people who are hurting and broken (for whatever reason) need its support.

It's hard for me to see where God has been in all this. I've been a Christian for over 20 years, and I almost abandoned my faith. I guess if any good has come from it, it would be that I have had to confront my own issues of rejection, fear and the need for rescue. It has also caused me to re-evaluate my beliefs, which has meant a deepening relationship with Jesus.

I haven't got there yet, and I'm still working through issues around my marriage breakdown. But I know that each step I take in trusting the Lord, the closer I move towards wholeness in him.

I thank him for that!

Together

Revelation and recovery: a wife's story

I knew practically nothing about homosexuality when my husband of ten years told me the shocking truth: that he would prefer to be in a relationship with a man. He hadn't "acted out" or been unfaithful to me in practice, but I wasn't what he wanted. I felt like the poor consolation prize. Due to his Christian values he knew he wasn't permitted what he really wanted, a gay relationship, so I was better than nothing. Prior to this I had believed we were happily married. However, my husband was just acting the role of the devoted husband. It was a facade to hide the truth. His Christian life was also almost a sham. He went through the motions of being a committed Christian, but in reality he was practically spiritually dead.

I had to learn about homosexuality the hard way, as someone who has been devastated by it. I don't claim to be an expert on this topic. Although my husband's revelation occurred nearly two years ago, most of my energy has been spent on grieving and trying to put the pieces of my life back together.

I also don't claim to be objective. I'm far too involved for that. However, I am confident that I now know far more about homosexuality than the average churchgoer. Ignorance can be, and often is, harmful. Ignorance causes many Christians who struggle with unwanted same-sex attraction to suffer in despair and silence instead of seeking help. Then when some seek help they are given incorrect and damaging advice due to ignorance.

Ignorance leads Christians to condemn without compassion. Ignorance means that those, like me, who have been hurt by someone else's homosexual struggle, aren't equipped to deal with the problem and don't know where to turn. There is so much shame, embarrassment and misunderstanding surrounding this issue that many suffer completely alone.

To assist in removing some of this ignorance, I would like to dispel some of the myths about homosexuality that abound in our Christian community. I should make it clear that this article only focuses on males with same-sex attraction, not females struggling with these issues.

Myth #1: Gays are born not made

Gays are made, not born. Despite what the media would like us to believe, there is no proof of a link between genes or hormones and homosexual orientation. Neither do homosexuals choose to be attracted to the same sex. In most cases, they become that way inclined largely due to the sins of others.

The histories of most homosexual men are amazingly similar. There is usually an emotionally distant, harsh or physically absent father. The little boy never feels loved and accepted by his father and often grows up hating his father or feeling indifferent towards him. Sometimes, the mother also contributes to the problem. She may be emotionally dependent on her son (particularly if the husband is not providing for her emotional needs). The little boy develops an unhealthy affinity with his mother and identifies with her more than with his father. He may know that his mother wanted a daughter and so he unconsciously assumes that role. His parents do usually love him, but he may be oversensitive to the imperfections in the family relationships. (Remember, of course, that I am speaking generally and this may not fit with every situation). In early adolescence (or even before) there is usually sexual contact with a male. Normally the boy is the victim of abuse by an older teenage "friend" or a man he knows and trusts. So the boy's first sexual experience is with a male.

The boy takes into adulthood unresolved hurts and unmet needs. His need for same-sex love and approval is normal and natural, but these needs were not met at the critical time. This hunger for male love becomes transmuted into sexual attraction.

Myth #2: Marriage is the solution

Wrong, wrong, wrong! I'm sorry, but this myth is too close to home for me to be anything but emphatic about it. And this is not just my personal experience. Since the foundation of the problem is a need for same-sex love that wasn't provided in the critical growing years, opposite-sex love does not cure the problem. For a couple of years, the husband may genuinely believe he is cured as his "in-love" feelings overshadow all else. However, after this honeymoon, the husband finds himself back at square one. He may even struggle more than ever before, as the pressures of financial and family responsibility cause him to seek relief. Many homosexual men confess to their wives after about ten years of marriage. Many act out their homosexuality for the first time in their lives after they marry.

99

When my husband was around 20 years old, he was so desperate and depressed that he overcame his shame and told his minister his problem. His minister then referred him to the local Christian psychologist. This professional psychologist told my husband that he needed to find a girlfriend. He was told that things would sort themselves out once he was in a heterosexual relationship. Such misguided advice has had serious consequences. As well as many more years of unnecessary struggling in silence, there are now other lives at stake. My life and the lives of our children are now directly affected by my husband's choices. It would have been so much easier for him, and far less painful for me, if he had dealt with his homosexuality as a young single. He needs time to work on his issues, but with a busy job, a wife and children, and a house to maintain, when does he have the time?

Myth #3: If you don't practise, you aren't really homosexual

Some people think that a person is only homosexual if they live the actively homosexual life. The argument goes like this: If I want to ski, that doesn't make me a skier. I would only call myself a skier if I actually skied. However, to be consistent with this argument, you would have to say that heterosexuals are only heterosexuals if they are sexually active. These words describe sexual orientation and feeling. 'Heterosexual' means 'attracted to the opposite sex' and 'homosexual' means 'attracted to the same sex', whether practising or not.

Some of those involved in ministry to men with unwanted same-sex attraction are reluctant to use the word 'homosexual', as they believe it is an unhelpful label which implies much more than just sexual orientation. I am not disagreeing with that approach. However, I think it is dangerous and incorrect to draw a black and white distinction between orientation and action. For example, a young man goes to his minister for help because he is struggling with homosexual feelings, although he has never been sexually active. If the minister believes the first argument he may reassure the man that as long as he doesn't sin he doesn't really have a problem. After all, we are all tempted in different ways and this is just his particular temptation. The minister does not take the problem seriously, the young man is not given help and he continues in despair.

Myth #4: Homosexuality is just like any other sin

In one sense, of course, this is right. Homosexual sin is no worse than any other sin in God's eyes. God hates all sin. However, homosexuality is different to your everyday, run-of-the-mill sin because it is so consuming. It is more like alcoholism. It is a destructive slavery which affects every aspect of a man's life. It robs a man of his masculine identity and self-esteem. It robs him of close, supportive, normal male friendships. It robs him of normal feelings and attractions to women. It destroys a man's relationship with God. It makes his life a perpetual battle and he feels he is always defeated.

Myth #5: You would know if you lived with a homosexual

Homosexual men in Christian circles live the double life. They may be involved with and apparently committed to church, but they are really a slave to this sin. They have perfected the art of hiding their secret through a lifetime of practice. Usually parents, and even wives, have no idea their loved one has such feelings. That's why the revelation is usually such an enormous shock.

The Road to Recovery

Since homosexual men are made, not born, they can be remade. However, it is a long, slow, difficult process for most men. It involves undoing a lifetime of attitudes and replacing them with new ones. For some it involves breaking a very real addiction to sin. Since a lack of appropriate same-sex love and approval is the core of the problem, this is where much of the change has to occur. Men trying to escape from homosexual feelings need to develop close, normal male friendships to provide what they have needed all their lives. They need to grow in confidence that they can relate to the average man and that they will be accepted, not rejected. These men usually need to address their attitudes and feelings to their fathers. They need to change the way they view themselves and become more confident of their masculine identity. Healing also involves disclosure. Sin thrives in the darkness of secrecy but has trouble surviving the light of truth and confession. Men with unwanted homosexual feelings need to learn to be more open, honest and accountable. Counsellors and support groups are important for this process.

What I have given is a simplified picture of complex issues. Hopefully, though, it provides a basic sketch of the road to recovery.

Compassion

Understanding the cause of homosexuality should lead us to deep compassion for these men. I must say now, though, that this is the part I feel least qualified to comment on. I have taken my husband's homosexuality so personally, as a direct rejection of me, that I still find it somewhat difficult to try to look objectively at what my husband is experiencing. So I won't pretend to understand what it is like to be struggling with homosexuality.

Those affected, like my husband, describe their struggle as living in a private hell. It's like being desperately thirsty but not being allowed to drink. It's also similar to an alcoholic trying to give up his alcohol. There's the constant fighting within yourself, the constant feeling of failure, the constant guilt, the feeling of being powerless to change, and the constant despair. It affects the man's relationship with God. He might feel the fight is useless and give in. Feelings of deep guilt may make a close relationship with God almost impossible. Or he may be angry with God for not answering his prayer to take this struggle away.

Homosexual men definitely aren't 'gay' individuals. They have carried their childhood wounds and needs into adulthood, and normally have low self-esteem. As Christians we need to have compassion for these people and offer our acceptance, whilst not condoning their lifestyle.

Conclusions

1. If you are a Christian man who has unwanted homosexual feelings, seek help now. You don't have to be the slave of this sin all your life. There is hope. You can change, but only with professional help.

2. If you have a loved one who is homosexual, you probably need help too. There is so much embarrassment and misunderstanding about this issue that the average person may not know how to deal with your situation. You need specialised help from people who really understand. They can support you.

3. Young women, do not marry a man with any history of homosexual involvement or feelings unless he has first had long-term professional help and has changed his orientation. You can't cure him.

4. If you do not fall into one of the above categories:

- Become informed. You can have someone from an organization such as Liberty come and speak at your church. Liberty will give you an honest, compassionate and Christ-centred view of homosexual issues. They can also provide some excellent brochures, books and videos.
- Be compassionate and supportive of those fellow believers who struggle with homosexual feelings. The homosexual desperately needs 'straight' friends, so instead of retreating, support him. Just be a genuine friend and show your concern.
- Be compassionate and supportive of those who have been hurt by someone else's homosexuality. These people will probably be grieving. They may also feel very angry and/or very guilty. They need comfort, support and a shoulder to cry on. Their pain may be great.

Learning a new way: a husband's story

A bad beginning

I was a small, shy, sensitive, 'nice' boy. I was very good at home, I was very good at school, I was very good at church. I was too good and too nice. My father was distant, always seemed angry and impatient, was at times violent and was probably alcoholic. At a very early age I began to hate my father for how he treated my mother, and I resolved firmly that I was never going to be like him. Today I know that this was defensive detachment. My mother (whom I loved fiercely and lived to please) was devoted to me. Being a bright boy, she confided in me and found the comfort in her relationship with her son that she could not find in her husband. It was a classic co-dependant relationship and more of a burden than a little boy should have been asked to bear, but I did so willingly.

As I grew a little older, I had difficulty making friends, especially with boys. When I had male friends, they were 'nerdy' types, like me. I spent more time with the girls and stayed out of the way of the rough boys. Being small and shy, I was bullied at various times.

When I was somewhere between eight and ten, I met a single elderly man who was lonely and drank far too much. We were two outcasts who had no other friends. For me, the man was a father figure who had time for me and accepted me. As the relationship developed, the man introduced a sexual element, perhaps entrenching in me something I had suspected for some time: I was attracted to other boys and men, not girls.

From bad to worse

As I grew into and past adolescence, the same-sex attraction strengthened and solidified. I never acted out, more due to fear and lack of opportunity than any great self-control. I suffered in silence. Nobody knew, nobody could know. I was a Christian, but there was a deep, dark place that I generally kept God out of. The guilt, the pain, the unfulfilled longing and the loneliness were difficult to bear, but what choice did I have? I prayed and prayed to God to take away my homosexual orientation and loneliness, but it didn't happen.

Eventually, in desperation, I confided in my minister. The minister was sympathetic and referred me to a counsellor. But the counselling sessions were unhelpful and I soon ended them. An opportunity lost. I know now that the earlier these issues are dealt with the better.

By the time I was about 23, I was desperately lonely and depressed. I knew that I could not stay single as I couldn't bear the loneliness, but I also knew that a homosexual relationship was out of the question. It was either suicide or get married. So I began to look for a wife. I started to go out with a beautiful young woman from church. Early in the marriage everything was great and I thought I might finally have overcome my problems. Various children came along. Eventually however, all the problems resurfaced.

Even as a physically mature male, my sense of self-identity and masculinity was almost non-existent. Inside, I was still that little boy who stopped growing up all those years ago when I rejected my father, as he rejected me. I have forgiven my father and have actively sought to be reconciled to him, but even now he is unable to give the little I ask for. Perhaps his parting comment to me sums up the gulf between our expectations: "I gave you a roof over your head and some nice holidays and no-one can expect more than that". But even if we are reconciled, I know that I cannot regain as an adult what I lost as a child. We must forgive (and seek forgiveness), grieve and move on.

If you see or know young boys like I was (especially in your own family), take action if you can. If the father is often away or absent, emotionally distant, angry or suchlike I get worried. If the boy is quiet, over-sensitive, plays with girls rather than boys, is awkward at sport and generally lacking confidence, I get even more worried. Act before it is too late. If the boy is yours, fathers (or uncles), love him and tell him you love him, spend time with him, hug him, do 'boy things' with him. My father has never hugged me in my life, and has certainly never told me he loved me. What simple things can make all the difference. Having learnt the hard way, I now spend time with my son and tell him every day that I love him. And he knows I mean it. He is growing into a happy confident boy and is my delight. We men can break the cycle.

Why am I writing?

However, I write this article mainly to encourage those who are struggling with same-sex attraction to go on in that struggle. FOR YOUR OWN HAPPINESS AND FUTURE, DO NOT GIVE UP!!! These days, my fantasies about the 'gay' life have been well and truly shattered. Instead of viewing the gay lifestyle as the fulfilment of everything I longed for, I see in many homosexual men deep-seated emotional immaturity and insecurity, major self-identity issues, unbridled hedonism, sexual addiction, rampant promiscuity, fleeting unsatisfying relationships, AIDS, STDs, drugs, chronic depression and great loneliness when the bloom of youth is gone. Life is far from 'gay', and these are not the building blocks for 'happily ever after'. Homosexuality is not part of God's plan and whatever we do which is not part of God's plan inevitably leads to failure.

Rock bottom

Resuming my story: a few years ago I told my wife that I was gay, that I wasn't attracted to her any more and that I wasn't sure I loved her any more. My Christian life was basically dead. You can imagine the pain and grief I caused. Of course, I hadn't told her of my renewed struggle. One thing I've noticed about people like me is that we are very good at hiding things. We are our own worst enemies.

Things had reached rock bottom. I was thinking of leaving and my wife was thinking of throwing me out if I didn't do something. I confess that much of the impetus for my progress has come from my wife's ideas rather than my own initiative. I often resented her 'helpful suggestions' at the time, but her persistence has saved me and our marriage. Of course, I know that this passivity is so much a feature of the homosexually oriented.

It is something I continue to struggle with.

The (long) road to recovery

I am still on the road to recovery. My first step was to start reading, to understand why I was like I was. I went to the local Christian bookstore and surreptitiously scanned the titles. I still like *You Don't Have To Be Gay*.[16] It was a simple message I needed to hear and believe. But Alan Medinger's book *Growth Into Manhood*[17] is unquestionably the best I have ever read as it focuses on the reorientation process. There are lots of other good titles.

As part of this process, my wife sacrificially 'gave' me Saturday mornings to myself to investigate the issues and spend time with God. I knew that I had to take time out of my busy life to find out who I was and to escape the cycle. As time went on, I learned that I was a copybook case. All the predispositions and environmental factors were there.

The next stage after reading the books was to see a counsellor—another daunting step for someone like me who was so secretive. It took a while, but eventually, and with encouragement from my wife, I went to see a counsellor who specializes in these problems. Speaking with others is very important to break the cycle of secrecy and sin.

After a year in counselling, I was finally able to let go of the sadness and pain which had dominated my life and drained most of my emotional reserves. With encouragement from my counsellor, I poured out my heart and pain to God, often in tears and emotional agony and without words, as I knew God understood. There came a day when the pain was all gone, and from there my road to recovery accelerated. I can still feel the pain, but as a memory, not a reality. I have learnt that we have to deal with the emotions. Holding them in is destructive and hinders healing. Without all the pain, I linger less in self pity, another trap which hinders healing.

Next, I confided in a close safe friend about my orientation issues. My friend was open and concerned, but has been unable to offer much ongoing support. He has too many of his own issues to deal with in a busy life. I realise now that I had unrealistic expectations, but being prepared to talk to my friend was an important step in coming out of my comfort zone.

After I had been in counselling for some time, I joined a support group with Liberty Christian Ministries. I am still in the support group and find it invaluable in many ways: worshipping God, learning about the causes and treatments for homosexuality, sharing deep hurts and suffering in a safe environment and being encouraged by other 'strugglers'. I also pray for all the group members daily, as I know they pray for me.

The keys to recovery

In my experience there are two keys to recovery. The first thing I had to do was to get my relationship with God right. I had to cling to him and pour out my heart and concerns. I have learned to love him as I never have before. I spend regular time with him in prayer and Bible reading, and I am involved in church and Bible study groups. I am far from perfect in this area, but in the last few years I have learned to know God in a deeper way. I have let him into that dark secret place, and its hold over me is broken.

The second key is obedience and holiness, and they go hand in hand with clinging to God. It is very difficult to have a close relationship with God if you are engaged in active sin, and also difficult to be engaged in active sin if you have a close relationship with God. During a Liberty support group meeting we were watching a video by Sy Rogers, a leading speaker in this area. He said "It is better to suffer for doing what is right than for doing what is wrong". These words burned into my heart and I resolved to adopt them as my motto. In desperation, I set myself some absolute boundaries to turn the tide on sin: look at a man only once (on the street, on the bus, at work) for temptation soon turns to lust; no watching SBS after ten at night (there's just too much sexually explicit material); there are a couple of others.

For those of you who are strugglers, you will know your danger points. Identify them and stay away from them. Pray every day for strength and let the Holy Spirit do his work. Listen to his promptings. And if you fail, repent and start again. God always forgives the penitent. I have learnt from painful experience that all the rationalizations in the world don't lead to healing. What is needed is firm, decisive action in partnership with God. Holiness may hurt sometimes, but it beats guilt and depression any day.

Since adopting my fairly simple rules, I have noticed radical improvements in my life. The orientation is still there, but it is less dominating. I find it easier to resist temptation. Resistance and small successes lead to greater confidence and ever-strengthening determination and optimism.

Another thing I have noticed is that my path to healing has not been linear. I reach a particular level and stay there for a while, almost as if building energy for the next leap. Then I make the next leap and plateau for a while and so on. Some of the plateaus have lasted for some time, while others have lasted for a short time. The speed of the leaps seems to be increasing. No doubt the path to healing is very different for all of us. Don't be discouraged if you seem to have plateaued. Pray that God will show you the keys to your next leap. You will be amazed at how often he does.

Where am I now?

My story is still in the making. I am by no means free of homosexual attractions, but I have come a long way. I made a resolution with myself some years ago, when I began this journey, that I wanted to be free of homosexuality by the time I was 40. I didn't kid myself that an instant fix was going to happen, although I know God could do it if he chose to. I have made good progress, and I have time yet to achieve my goal. Even if I don't, I know I will have reached a point where life is enjoyable and satisfying, rather than intolerable as it once was. I am happy with my life, but I have a sense that God has even better in store.

So where to from here? For me, more God and more obedience. I am also trying to work on some deeper, healthy relationships with other men and 'doing the things men do'. Like it or not, if you want to play in the man's game, you have to play by the men's rules. Sometimes this means doing things I am not really interested in, but over time I am learning that I can become interested in things that never appealed before (all part of my defensive detachment from my father I think—anything he liked, by definition, I didn't).

With encouragement from my counsellor, I have written myself a mission statement which covers God, church, family, work and me. My overarching approach is a change in attitude. It is encapsulated by the statement 'live in love not fear'. It means being free to be who I am and caring less what others think; being free to succeed—and to fail; and being free to live life in a giving way, but also being free to set boundaries with others, in love. I find it hard to live this way consistently, but it's liberating when I do, and I am constantly working at it.

And what of my wife and me? Over the years that have followed since my revelations, my wife and I have had many painful encounters. We have seen a marriage counsellor and benefited greatly from this. My wife has forgiven me for the great pain I caused her. It grieves me still. Today, our relationship is much stronger and deeper. But I must be careful not to take that relationship for granted. Constant attention is required.

We are not responsible for what happened to us as children, but we are responsible for how we live as adults. I have learnt, painfully, that God's way is best. God calls us to choose faithfulness, knowing that only in relationship with him is there true happiness. If we focus on him and trust his love with obedience, great things are possible. I face the future with optimism and hope: that certain hope that belongs to those who love him.

Notes

1 Joe Dallas, *Desires in Conflict: Answering the Struggle for Sexual Identity*, Harvest House Publishers, 1991, p. 117.

2 John Stott, *New Issues Facing Christians Today*, Marshall Pickering, 1999 (first published in 1984) p. 402.

3 Joseph Nicolosi, *Reparative Therapy Of Male Homosexuality*, Jason Aronson Inc., 1991, p. 111.

4 Thomas E. Schmidt, *Straight & Narrow? Compassion & Clarity in the Homosexuality Debate*, IVP, Illinois, 1995, p. 108.

5 John Stott, *Same Sex Partnerships*, Marshall Pickering, 1998, Preface.

6 Earl Wilson, *Counselling and Homosexuality*, Volume 15 of the Resources for Christian Counselling series, Word, 1988, p. 173.

7 Sy Rogers is an international speaker and teacher. His life story of recovery from homosexuality as well as transsexuality has been shared on six continents and in numerous media interviews and publications. It has been a wonderful testimony to the power of God to heal as well as an inspiration to many.

8 Briar Whitehead, *Craving For Love*, First published 1993, Monarch Publications, Kent, England. Whitehead Associates, Lower Hutt, New Zealand. Revised and reprinted, 2001.

9 Henry Cloud and John Townsend, *Boundaries: When to say YES, When to say NO, to Take Control of your Life*, Strand Publishing, 1992.

10   Mario Bergner, *Setting Love In Order*, Hamewith Books, an imprint of Baker Book House Company, 1995.

11   Jeanette Howard, *Out Of Egypt*, Monarch Publications, 1991, p.125.

12   Jeffrey Satinover, *Homosexuality and the Politics of Truth*, Baker Books, 1996.

13   Mel White, *Stranger At The Gate*, Simon & Schuster, 1994.

14   John Shelby Spong, *Living In Sin?*, Harper, 1988.

15   See note 2.

16   Jeff Konrad, *You Don't Have To Be Gay*, Monarch Publications, 1993.

17   Alan Medinger, *Growth Into Manhood*, WaterBrook Press, 2000.

Appendices

APPENDIX 1

How we went gay

Tony Payne

Over the past generation, the public profile of homosexuality has changed enormously. In the 1960s, a public figure who openly declared that he was gay, or spoke favourably of homosexuality in some way, would have been treated at the very least with suspicion, and more probably as an outcast. Gay activism has changed that. Now, the homosexual community is openly recognized.

Gay has become part of the mainstream. Almost without our realising it, Western society has been transformed in its attitude towards homosexuality—from deep suspicion and condemnation, through tolerance, to open acceptance and promotion of its benefits.

The story of this transformation is worth telling, so much so that in the course of this article I will tell it twice: once in its popular version, and once in light of facts that are now becoming known. Of course, it will be a very abbreviated history—more a highlights package than a history—but I trust an instructive one nevertheless.

The usual story

For many gay and lesbian activists, the gay rights movement began one warm summer night in 1969 in lower Manhattan. On that evening, New York police raided the Stonewall Bar, aiming to arrest patrons engaged in (what were then illegal) homosexual acts. It was not the raid that was so significant— it was the fact that, for the first time, the gays fought back. A metal garbage can was thrown through a police car window, and a mini-riot ensued. *Stonewall*, as it simply became known, became a powerful symbol for gay militancy throughout the 70s and 80s.

Stonewall may have been the spark that set the movement alight, but fuel for the fire had been laid down well before. In the late 1940s, a respectable 53-year old former entomologist (his specialty was the gall wasp) published a fat scientific study that *Life* Magazine declared to be the most sensational and popular scientific work published since Darwin's *Origin of the Species*. The work was entitled *Sexual Behaviour in the Human Male,* and its chief author was Dr Alfred Kinsey.

The Kinsey Report, as it came to be known, was revolutionary not simply because of its size and comprehensiveness, but because it lifted the lid on sexual taboos and behaviour that Americans had previously been reluctant to discuss. Kinsey (and his co-authors Pomeroy and Martin) surveyed a massive sample of Americans and reported that 90% of males masturbated, 85% had engaged in premarital intercourse, 30-45% had conducted extra-marital sexual relationships, and around 70% had visited prostitutes. Furthermore, Kinsey contended that 37% of males had experienced homosexual orgasm post-pubity, and that 10%

of the population were predominately homosexual.[1]

The implications of Kinsey's research were not lost on the American public. If, for example, 10% of the population were homosexual (which was how the figures were popularly represented), then homosexuality was no longer a deviant criminal act ('sodomy') only practised by a very small number of social outcasts. It ought now to be recognized as the fairly common behaviour of a large minority. Homosexual activists cite Kinsey as the man who made the modern gay movement possible.[2]

Kinsey's research found a receptive audience in the socially and sexually volatile 60s and 70s. With baby boomers in droves discovering the joys of making love not war, the time was certainly right for a counter-cultural cause like the gay rights movement to be born. It was not only the age of Aquarius, but the age of the pleasure principle ('if it feels good, do it'), the age of self-determination and rebellion against repressive hierarchies and authority, the age of Me.

In this climate of personal and sexual revolution, the American Psychiatric Association made a crucial decision. In 1973, it removed homosexuality from its list of psychiatric disorders, and reclassified it as a 'condition', much like left-handedness. It was official. Homosexuality was no longer to be regarded as something that was 'wrong with you'. It was not an illness or a disorder to be cured; it was simply the way some people happened to be.

1. More specifically, Kinsey found that 10% of his sample had been "more or less exclusively" homosexual for at least three years between the ages of 16 and 55.
2. See Mark Thompson (ed), *The Long Road To Freedom* (New York: St Martin's Press, 1994), pp. 22, 59-60, 102, 164, cited in J. Reisman, 'Kinsey and the Homosexual Revolution' in George A. Rekers (ed.), *The Journal of Human Sexuality* (Carollton: Lewis and Stanley, 1996), p.21.

Some 20 years later, this judgement was only further con-
firmed by two studies that were widely reported as demon-
strating a genetic or biological basis for homosexuality. In
1991, Simon LeVay published an article in *Science* magazine
reporting that he had discovered a cluster of cells in the brain
of homosexual men that was different from those in heterosexual men. Two years later, another study was published in
Science, this time claiming that evidence had been found of a
genetic variation on the X chromosome that was associated
with homosexuality. The mainstream media's response to
these studies was to run headlines like "Research points
toward gay gene". The perception that had become increasingly common in the 70s and 80s was decisively reinforced in
the public mind—namely, that homosexuality was simply
something you were born with, that you could either deny it
or acknowledge it, but that you could not escape it.

During this whole period, popular culture was also playing
an important role in the normalization of homosexuality. It
both reflected and encouraged the increasing respectability of
all things homosexual. In mainstream film, there began to
develop the stereotype of the loving gay couple who had a
stronger and more lasting relationship than the heterosexual
couples in the story—as in *4 Weddings And A Funeral* and *Mrs
Doubtfire*. Other films carried a more self-consciously gay
agenda, such as *The Sum Of Us, Priscilla: Queen Of The Desert*
and the academy award winning *Philadelphia*. Gay issues and
events began to migrate from subculture magazines and newspapers to the mainstream dailies. Advocacy of gay causes
appeared to become standard editorial policy in major metro-
politan newspapers throughout the Western world.

At the same time, gay activists lobbied fiercely for homosexual behaviour to be decriminalized. In many jurisdictions they

were successful, and some even managed to have legislation passed protecting gays and lesbians from 'vilification'.

The transformation of the Sydney Gay and Lesbian Mardi Gras from a minority fringe protest march to a dominant cultural event is perhaps the most potent symbol of the change that has occurred in the last 20-30 years. It is widely reported that over 500,000 people come to witness the parade. It is portrayed as not only a celebration of Sydney's acceptance of its homosexual community, but a demonstration of the vibrancy of that community and the positive contribution it has to make to the life of the city—as seen not only in the month-long arts festival that is now part of the Mardi Gras, but in the millions of tourist dollars that the event pulls in.

In 2001, to be gay is to be on the cutting edge, to be hip, to be an individual, to be part of the glitzy yet sensitive culture that represents all that is best in humanity's evolving nature.

The untold story

There is another side to most stories, especially those whose currency and power exist in the mainstream media. In popular culture, certain statements or ideas come to have a life of their own. They assume a legitimacy and truthfulness merely by virtue of their being repeated often enough.

The normalization of homosexuality is one such story. A host of popular cliches, statistics, perceptions and platitudes about gayness have entered our culture, and become widely accepted. It is now commonplace to say that gays are 'born that way', that loving faithful gay couples exist in significant numbers and ought to be granted all the legal rights of heterosexual couples, that to be gay is to be exciting and to lead a liberated lifestyle, and so on.

When Christians attempt to discuss the subject of homosexuality, we do so in this context. In this sort of climate, to express a view that is in any sense negative regarding homosexual behaviour or the homosexual lifestyle, takes considerable courage. It takes the courage of one's own convictions, that homosexuality is fundamentally against God's purposes, despite the apparent groundswell of opinion in its support. And it takes courage to withstand the abuse and ridicule that follows any expression of opinion to this effect.

However, it may serve to strengthen our weak arms and feeble knees to realise that much of the story we have been relating so far in this article is not as it seems. As a society, we have been gravely misled. And the story of the deception starts with Kinsey.

It is now apparent that Alfred Kinsey was something other than a disinterested, unbiased scientific observer of America's sexual mores. Recent biographical research has shown Kinsey himself was a homosexual, and a masochist (in the sexual sense) who, as he grew older, pursued an interest in extreme forms of sexuality, with an increasing compulsiveness. At the time of his famous report, Kinsey had begun conducting (and participating in) sexual experiments in his attic, filming members of his staff having sex with each other, and with his wife, and also filming exhibitions of gay sex, especially of the sadomasochistic variety.[3]

Kinsey, there seems little doubt, had powerful personal reasons for pursuing sex research, and for attempting to demonstrate that there was no such thing as 'deviancy'. It led him to scientific sleight-of-hand, if not outright fraud. The details of

3.   This is the verdict of Kinsey's most recent biographer, James H. Jones; writing for *The Australian Magazine*, Nov 22-23, 1997. His biography is entitled, *Alfred C. Kinsey: A Public/Private Life*, published by Norton, 1997.

Kinsey's work have since been seriously undermined. Judith Reisman is one of a number of recent critics who argue that Kinsey's research was both fraudulent and criminal.[4] His sample of American males, although large, was hardly representative of the population as a whole. 26% of Kinsey's subjects, for example, were 'sex offenders'; 25% were in prison; among the rest, pimps, male prostitutes and frequenters of 'gay bars' were over-represented. There is little doubt that sexually promiscuous males, especially homosexuals, were massively over-represented in Kinsey's sample, but this is something that Kinsey repeatedly denied or attempted to obscure. Thus Kinsey's contention that 10% of the population is predominately homosexual is a massive exaggeration. A barrage of more recent studies have put the figure at around 1% for men, and less than half that for women—and this after 30 years of gay activism to make being homosexual a socially acceptable lifestyle.[5]

Indeed, homosexual activists now admit that the populist 10% figure drawn from Kinsey was a convenient exaggeration:

> The thing about the 'one in ten'—I think people probably always did know that it was inflated. But it was a nice number that you could point to, that you say 'one in ten', and it's a really good way to get people to visualise that we're here.[6]

---

4. Reisman, *op cit.*
5. For a summary of these studies see Andrew Shead 'Homosexuality and the church: history of the debate' in B.G.Webb (ed.), *Theological and Pastoral Responses to Homosexuality* (Adelaide: Openbook, 1994). Also see J. Dallas, 'Responding to Pro-Gay Theology' in *The Journal of Human Sexuality*, p. 79.
6. A lesbian activist member of ACT-UP, quoted in 'Responding to Pro-Gay Theology', *ibid.*, p. 79.

The deception does not stop there. At the time, the decision of the American Psychiatric Association in 1973 to 'declassify' homosexuality appeared to be the impartial decision of progressive enlightened scientists based on their professional expertise. However, it has subsequently become clear that the decision was made not because of any new scientific evidence, or as part of a disinterested search for truth, but through a systematic campaign of political action on the part of gay activists. Indeed, at a crucial point in the debate, a letter was mailed by influential psychiatrists within the association to over 30,000 members of the APA, urging them to support the change. It was not revealed at the time that the letter was drafted and funded by the National Gay Task Force.[7]

As for the recent scientific studies that have claimed that homosexuality is basically genetic or biological in origin, here too there has been exaggeration, shoddy methodology and rampant spin-doctoring in the interests of advancing the cause. The studies themselves have come under severe criticism from other scientists in the field, not only for their methodology but for the fallacious manner in which conclusions have been drawn from them. Simon LeVay's study concerning differences in cell biology in the brains of homosexual males, for example, suffered from two basic flaws. Firstly, since the subjects in his studies were all dead (the information was collected from autopsies), there was no way of determining the sexual behaviour of the subjects with

7. Jeffrey Satinover provides all the details, as well as further examples, in his book *Homosexuality and the Politics of Truth* (Grand Rapids: Baker, 1996), pp. 31-40. He also has a helpful discussion of the complexities of defining homosexuality as an 'illness' when it might be more accurately described as a damaging behaviour pattern. Also see C. Socarides, 'How America Went Gay' in *The Journal of Human Sexuality*, pp. 29-32.

any reliability. Secondly, and more significantly, even if the subjects with different clusters of cells did engage in homosexual behaviour, there is no logical reason to regard the different brain structure as causative of the behaviour. It may be associated with the behaviour, but this could be in a number of ways: it could *result* from the behaviour (since we know that the brain does lay down new cell structures as a result of particular activities); or it could be associated with some traits or characteristics that are common among homosexual men without being causative of the homosexuality.[8]

These subtleties, it hardly needs to be said, did not stand in the way of a good media story. It was much simpler, and more appealing, simply to trumpet the finding that homosexuality was genetic, that it was as good as proved, and that homosexuality was therefore a perfectly normal and acceptable variant of human behaviour. It was just another area in which modern science had liberated us from the primitive, irrational and oppressive superstitions of Christian dogma.

It was an important victory for the gay lobby, because research had shown them that if people could be persuaded that homosexuality was largely genetic or biological in origin, they would be much more likely to be accepting of it.[9] The volume of stories in the popular media between 1991 and 1994 based largely around the two most famous studies (of LeVay and Hamer) did this for the gay lobby.

The only problem, of course, was that the studies in question proved very little, and certainly did not even begin to

8. For a more detailed discussion of these issues, see Appendix 2, below.
9. K. E. Ernulf, S. M. Innala, and F. L. Whitam, 'Biological Explanation, Psychological Explanation, and Tolerance of Homosexuals: A Cross-National Analysis of Beliefs and Attitudes', *Psychological Reports* 65 (1998), pp. 1003-10, quoted in Satinover, *op. cit.*

demonstrate a genetic cause for homosexuality. Like the frequent quoting of the Kinsey figures, however, it seems that it is repetition that matters, not truth. The same can be said for the oft-quoted statistic that 500,000 people attend the Gay and Lesbian Mardi Gras each year (the figure of 700,000 has even been bandied around). Critics of the Mardi Gras have pointed out what a fantastically exaggerated figure this is, given the length of the route (only 3 km). Even if there was 10 metres available on each side of the parade the whole way, and spectators were crammed in uniformly at two people per square metre, that would yield a maximum of only 120,000 in attendance. One wonders how many are really there each year.

Wild exaggeration, propagandizing, backroom political deals, dodgy research, blatant lies. The story of how our culture—at least at the level of popular discourse—has come to accept homosexuality as an entirely normal and acceptable form of behaviour is not a pretty picture. Less pretty still is the reality of the gay lifestyle as the most recent research is now revealing it.

Were we to believe the stereotype of the gay man, as portrayed in the popular media, we would see him as a happy, healthy, sophisticated individual, who now embraces and celebrates the truth about his sexuality, and lives in a loving, caring, permanent monogamous relationship with his faithful lover and friend. This, however, is as much a fiction as Kinsey's 10% or the 700,000 at the Mardi Gras.

One of the byproducts of gay activism has been a massive increase in research into the gay lifestyle over the last 15-20 years. In *Straight and Narrow?* Thomas Schmidt surveys the results of nearly 200 such studies, all of them conducted by reputable scientists and research facilities, and virtually all of them either positive or neutral in their attitude towards homosexuality. The results are almost too appalling to believe. As a lifestyle, homosexuality is extraordinarily dysfunctional and destructive, according to these studies. The stereotype of the happy gay man with his lifelong, loving partner is a myth. According to the research, the number of gay relationships that last at all past five years is so small as to be non-existent, and even of the small percentage of relationships that do last as long as five years, virtually none are monogamous.

Schmidt summarizes the findings of this vast body of recent research in an illustration, which is worth quoting at length:

> Suppose you were to move into a large house in San Francisco with a group of ten randomly selected homosexual men in their mid-thirties...[T]he relational and physical health of the group would look like this.
>
> Four of the ten are currently in relationships, but only one of those is faithful to his partner, and he will not be within a year. Four have never had a relationship that lasted more than a year, and only one has had a relationship that lasted more than three years. Six are having sex regularly with strangers, and the group averages almost two partners per person per month. Three of them occasionally take part in orgies. One is a sadomasochist. One prefers boys to men.
>
> Three of the men are currently alcoholics, five have a history of alcohol abuse, and four have a history of drug abuse. Three currently smoke cigarettes, five regularly use at least one illegal drug, and three are multiple drug users. Four have a history of acute depression, three have seriously contemplated suicide, and two have attempted suicide. Eight have a history of sexually trans-

mitted diseases, eight currently carry infectious pathogens, and three currently suffer from digestive or urinary ailments caused by these pathogens. At least three are HIV infected, and one has AIDS.[10]

It is worth repeating: these are not conclusions drawn from right-wing ideologues, or studies set up by Christians. The research that has yielded these astonishing results (or at least, astonishing to the modern mind) was quite secular, and in large measure positive towards homosexuality. Its unintended result is to paint a picture of the realities of the gay lifestyle that the spin doctors never reveal.

The same old story

It is interesting to reflect on how Christians handle shifts in popular sentiment and intellectual fashion. We usually lag behind the rest of society, perhaps out of an innate caution, perhaps because we are just slower to react, or perhaps (we might hope) because we wish to follow God's word rather than the world's wisdom. However, the sad truth is that we often trot obediently behind the latest shifts in contemporary thought, keeping a respectful distance of 10 or 15 years, but following all the same.

The pattern seems to be repeating itself with regard to homosexuality. The church is going gay, its re-evaluation of the orthodox Christian viewpoint being driven by the 'advances' of secular science and thought. Hermeneutical loopholes have been devised to evade the plain meaning of Scripture, and the crusade is now in full swing to achieve in the church the same normalization of homosexuality that has occurred in society as

10. T. Schmidt, *Straight and Narrow?* (Leicester: IVP, 1995), p.127.

a whole. Christian gay activists have learned from their secular counterparts the techniques of disturbing, unsettling and ultimately changing the attitudes of a community by capturing the minds of its opinion leaders.

As an illustration of this process, let us turn briefly to an open letter written by Bishop John Spong to the Primates of the Anglican Communion of the World. In this letter, Bishop Spong argues with great passion that it is time Christians stopped mistreating and demonizing homosexuals, and that we should wake up to the fact that we now live in the twentieth century. No-one believes anymore that homosexuality is a deviant, immoral behaviour. It is simply the way some people are born, and on this basis it is cruelly unjust and false to continue to discriminate against them in the church. Bishop Spong is on the extreme edge of those who would support the normalization of homosexuality within Christianity, but he nevertheless expresses with great clarity the issues in the debate. He expresses quite openly and without prevarication the forces that have led him to his position. He writes:

Our knowledge and understanding of homosexuality is changing: Over the last fifty years, dramatic new insights have been achieved in the studies of both human behaviour and the science of brain function. These insights have forced the Western world, led by medical and scientific people, to reject the wisdom of the past that viewed homosexuality as a choice rather than a given aspect of reality, as a mental illness rather than as part of the spectrum of human sexual activity, and as aberrant and evil behaviour engaged in by morally depraved people rather than a natural, albeit minority, part of humanity...

[He then cites the APA decision of 1973, and recent genetic and biological studies as mentioned above.]...

> The conclusion to which these data point is obvious; namely, homosexuality is a part of the human and biological norm. It is not an aberration or a sickness that needs to be overcome. These new insights, overwhelmingly accepted by the medical and scientific community, continue to be rejected, however, by uninformed religious people who buttress their attitude by appeals to a literal understanding of the Bible.

The force of the argument is quite clear. Science has led us to realise that homosexuality is really perfectly normal and innate in some people, and it is therefore sheer, blinkered, Bible-bashing prejudice to think otherwise.

It hardly needs to be said that Bishop Spong's argument contains the same kind of wild exaggeration and false claims of which the gay lobby has been repeatedly guilty. The vast majority of geneticists and 'medical people' do not accept that homosexuality is genetically or biologically determined. The evidence simply does not exist for that conclusion. The APA decision, as we have seen, was an act of political manipulation, not cool scientific debate.

The terrible irony is that Bishop Spong, and many others like him, argue for acceptance of homosexuality in the name of science and all that is modern and reasonable. Yet the very science which they seem to trust so implicitly is now telling us that homosexuality is a personal and social disaster. Could it be that what the Bible has been saying all along is true—that homosexual behaviour itself represents God's judgement on our foolish rebellion against him? That it is a violation of God's good created order; and that it leads only to deep harm?

If only Christians were a little further behind. If only we would wait long enough for the fads and fashions of the world's thinking to expend themselves and be proved faulty, then perhaps we could save ourselves the anguish of selling out the Bible in order to conform ourselves to the world.

It is true, of course, that not all Christians have so willingly embraced the normalization of gayness as Bishop Spong. There are those who see that the issue is (as always) about authority—whether we will be obedient to God as he speaks to us through the Scriptures, or listen to the siren call of alternative authorities, such as Experience ("but I know inside that I am gay") and Reason ("Science teaches us that there is nothing wrong with being gay").

There are growing signs of this resistance throughout the world—but that is yet another story.

APPENDIX 2

Is homosexuality biologically determined?

Dr Trevor Hunter

Introduction

On July 16 1993 the prestigious journal *Science* published a landmark study suggesting a possible genetic marker had been found for homosexuality. The public reporting of this finding was as widespread as it was hyperbolic. The *Wall Street Journal* titled it a Gay Gene.[1] *Time* magazine carried a lead article 'Born Gay'.[2] The findings were greeted with great enthusiasm by the wider gay community, and uncritically adopted by many. At the time of writing this article, a prominent Sydney lawyer engaged in a defamation suit has publicly stated of his homosexuality that he was 'born that way'.

1. *Wall Street Journal*, July 16, 1993.
2. July 15, 1993

Yet the biological causation of homosexuality as espoused by many, raises disturbing questions for the critical thinker, primarily about the way scientific data has been dealt with in the debate. The implied genetic determinism could ignite a major debate over the personal responsibility for sexual behaviour. Finally, what is to be made of those who claim to have left behind homosexual practice and have moved into stable heterosexual relationships? Gay activists assert such people don't exist, or were never gay in the first place, and that any claims to facilitate this sort of change are mistaken at best, or harmful and dangerous at worst.

This article explores some of these issues by considering the biological causation argument and looking at the evidence.

Incidence of Homosexuality

In 1995, the Queensland Institute of Medical Research[3] carried out a study of 5,000 sets of twins aged 19-59, and reported that 2.5 per cent of males and 1 per cent of females regarded themselves as exclusively homosexual.

This figure is in accord with most international studies on the incidence of homosexuality, with meta-analyses indicating figures ranging from 0.5 to 4 percent for men, and 0.25 to 1.2 per cent for women.[4] All studies identify a group that define themselves as neither exclusively heterosexual or homosexual, in that

---

3. As reported in the *The Sydney Morning Herald*, August 19, 1995.
4. Figures compiled by N. Whitehead in *My Genes Made Me Do It—A Scientific Look At Sexual Orientation*,(Lafayette: Huntingdon House, 1999), pp. 38ff. See also the ASCF study quoted by Prof. Philip Mitchell of 4.1% lifetime incidence of homosexual intercourse for males and 2.5% for females in B. G. Webb (ed.), *Theological and Pastoral Responses to Homosexuality*, (Adelaide: Open Book, 1994), p. 109.

a certain percentage feel some sexual attraction to members of the same sex as well as the opposite. The Queensland study indicated a figure of 10 per cent, while others have wide ranging figures depending on the methodology adopted by the authors, the method of recruitment and the framing of the questions.

Twin Studies

The impetus for positing a biological cause for homosexuality originally came from twin studies.

The above quoted study of Australian twins by the Queensland Institute of Medical Research analysed five thousand identical versus non-identical twins who were reared together and at home. The incidence of homosexuality was reported as 50 per cent higher in the former sub-group. Yet identical twins share the same or identical genetic material, so the concordance rate should have been 100 per cent if homosexuality is entirely a matter of genetics or biology. Moreover, there are methodological problems that need to be considered. Many studies were conducted on twins recruited through advertisements placed in gay and lesbian magazines, so the participants were self selecting. Most were not DNA-coded, so we only have the participants' word on whether they were identical or not. In most studies no questions were posed regarding ratio or intensity of homosexual to heterosexual feelings; rather, they were simply asked whether they were homosexual or heterosexual. Some have suggested that if there is a higher rate of homosexual behaviour in identical versus non-identical twins, it may be due to identical physical appearance, implying identical emotional and behavioural influences at work in their upbringing, although that hypothesis is yet to be proved.

Linkage Studies

Gene linkage studies are being performed as part of the Human Genome Project, a collaborative multinational research project that is aiming to unravel the base pairs coding for all genes on the 23 pairs of human chromosomes. Linkage studies take groups of families that seem to have a higher incidence than the general community of a particular disorder, such as Cystic Fibrosis or Huntingdon's Chorea. They also study conditions where there is a higher incidence in identical versus nonidentical twins. They analyze the subjects' chromosomes via sequencing with DNA markers, hoping to identify a consistent pattern in those who suffer these conditions, or in their relatives. Extended families with the diseases mentioned above have been studied, and DNA markers show a consistent pattern on individual chromosome regions that possibly correlate with genetic loci for these physical disorders.

The difficulty is greatly compounded when these methods are used to study behavioural characteristics in order to link them to a specific gene. Yet this is exactly what Dean Hamer attempted in a study of homosexuality in 40 pairs of gay brothers who also had a higher incidence of homosexuals than the general community on their mother's side—implying a possible X-linked transmission.[5] Using a series of known markers, he studied the X chromosome in these men and found a genetic sequence common to 33 cases of the 40 at the X q28 locus on the long arm of the X chromosome, providing evidence, he believed, of a clear linkage between this marker and transmission of homosexuality.

Although this study was widely publicized, the scepticism of

5.   Hamer *et al*, 'A linkage between DNA markers on the X chromosome and male sexual orientation', *Science*, 1993, 261, pp. 321-7.

the scientific community was not. Firstly, every attempt to define behavioural characteristics with a genetic disorder via linkage studies has failed, including manic depression, schizophrenia and alcoholism. This is highly significant, because doctors suspect there may be a biological influence in these diseases. Secondly, Hamer's study had no control group, so we don't know about the incidence of the detected abnormality in the normal population. Interlocutors have sought an explanation from Hamer as to why seven pairs of gay brothers did not have the abnormality detected. Many think the existence of bisexuality, or the homosexual attraction phase many adolescents go through, cannot be explained on this model, since genes work in an 'on-off' fashion. Others criticized the sample size, saying that the results did not reach statistical significance. Hamer himself stated that the importance of his ground-breaking work would be evidenced if the work could be reproduced by others. A number have tried,[6] without success.

Many in the gay community are not happy with this line of research, believing that it robs them of their freedom of choice with regard to their sexual identity. Some fear the concept of eugenics: that if the gay gene was found, then a way to remove it might also be sought. As a perceptive commentator with the benefit of hindsight has said by way of summation:

What is greeted with joy by the gay community are the findings which mean people can't help it, that they don't choose it... that therefore it must be natural. But if you

6. The latest is a Canadian study undertaken at the University of Western Ontario by Dr George Rice and published in 1999 in *Science*. The study was of 52 gay brothers using identical criteria to the Hamer study, yet no such genetic marker was found. It was publicised on the back pages as a small item in *The Sydney Morning Herald* on April 24, 1999 under the caption 'Gay gene thrown into doubt'.

think a behavioural gene could tell us anything about gay men in Australia in 1995 that is clearly an absurdity. You may be a bit predetermined to be a particular kind of person, but you also have to look at the kind of society that enables people to make certain sexual choices. Then you are still left with moral choices about your own behaviour.[7]

Anatomical/Structural Brain Differences

In 1991, neurologist Dr Simon Levay dissected the brains of 35 male cadavers, including 19 known homosexuals who had died of AIDS. His findings were published in the journal *Science*[8] where he concludes that a section of the brain in the hypothalamus designated INAH-3 was smaller in the homosexual men than in their heterosexual counterparts, and of a similar size to that of heterosexual women. The finding was considered significant, as there is some evidence from rat studies that structural differences in the hypothalamus may regulate their hormonal and behavioural differences. He used this evidence to argue for a biological basis for homosexuality.

However there are significant methodological problems with the study, and some have argued that Levay's findings may well have been caused by the disease process itself, rather than some other explanation. Most conclude that the sample size is too small to be of statistical significance, and would require replication with stricter controls for any tentative conclusions to be drawn.

Such a study was performed by Byne *et al* in a double blind

---

7. J. Hart, *The Sydney Morning Herald*, August 19, 1995.
8. S. Levay, 'A difference in hypothalamic structure between homosexual and heterosexual men', *Science*, 1991, 253, pp. 1034-7.

fashion, so that the researchers were unaware of the sexual orientation and practice of the cadavers dissected. The study did confirm a difference between the INAH-3 of men and women, but was unable to confirm a difference between homosexual and heterosexual men.[9] A number of other studies in other parts of the brain have been performed seeking to demonstrate anatomical or structural differences between homosexual and heterosexual people. To date nothing has been proven, and indeed after a literature search on the subject, one scientific reporter comments, "Neuroanatomists may yet find themselves handing the search for the roots of homosexuality back to the social psychologists and sociologists".[10]

Hormonal Differences

Many have argued that if there is a biological basis to homosexuality then it would be mediated hormonally, as this seems to be the case in animal studies.

Animal Studies

A number of studies have been performed on rats indicating that the reflex mounting behaviour of male rats is mediated by the testicular hormones. If a male rat is castrated at birth he is more likely to adopt the female receptive position, while female rats given testosterone at birth are more likely to perform male mounting positions during sexual stimulation. However there are significant difficulties in extrapolating these findings to humans—not the least of which is that human sexual activity is

9. Byne *et al*, 'Human sexual orientation: the biologic theories reappraised', *Archives of General Psychiatry*, 1993, 50, pp. 228-39.
10. G. Vines, 'Obscure origins of desire" *New Scientist*, 1992, 136, pp. 2-8.

motivated and not reflexive. Researchers have not been able to demonstrate discernable differences in androgenic (male) and oestrogenic (female) hormone levels between homosexual and heterosexual men and women.

Human Studies

A number of disorders affecting the developing human embryo would help us test the hypothesis that homosexuality may be mediated by insufficient male hormones (male homosexuality) or excessive female hormones (female homosexuality). In the absence of a Y chromosome, male hormones are not produced, and the embryo develops as a female. The Y chromosome is needed to produce testes that in turn release two major hormones. The Mullerian Inhibitory Factor (MIF) will suppress the development of female genitalia. Also testosterone will stimulate the development of external male genitalia.

• **Testicular Feminisation:** Here the embryo has the normal male genetic complement (XY) but lacks androgen receptors, so that the external genitalia are not responsive to the testosterone produced and therefore the infant at birth appears female and is reared as one. However, they lack a uterus and ovaries and thus fail to menstruate at pubity when investigations undertaken show they are genetically male. Their sex of rearing is female and so they develop sexual interests in males, despite normal XY chromosomes and male hormones.

• **Congenital Adrenal Hyperplasia:** Here the embryo has normal XX female chromosomes, with overactive adrenal glands producing an excess of hormones biochemically similar to testosterone. Consequently at birth they appear virilised, despite having a uterus and ovaries. If the condition is detected at birth and the enlarged clitoris is reduced, the child can be raised as a female. Despite having a higher level of male hormones, there is

no evidence of an increased incidence of female homosexuality.
• **Hormonally Treated Pregnancies:** Synthetic progesterones
(sex hormones) have been used in previous decades to prevent
miscarriages in pregnant women. The effects on the developing
foetus have been either masculinizing if the foetus is female, or
feminizing if the foetus is male. A number of studies have been
conducted on the subsequent sexual orientation of individuals
exposed to such hormone manipulation, but without conclusive
evidence of any effect.[11]

Conclusion: A Biological Contribution to Homosexuality?

At the present time there has been no definitive evidence presented to establish a biological cause for homosexuality despite
what the popular press may say. No gay gene has been discovered, and there are no posited biological pathways to explain
how such a gene or genes may work even if they did exist.
While geneticists, neuroanatomists, endocrinologists, and linkage and twin study researchers may not agree on a precise causation for homosexuality, they would be in broad agreement
that there is no such thing as genetic determinism.

Having said that, it is important to say that science has yet
to establish *any* human behaviour as genetically determined,
although it is possible that physical characteristics that are biologically given may influence later behaviour. People blessed
with a good visual acuity and physique may grow up to become
athletes or musicians or ballet artists, for each career requires
those same physical attributes. Indeed they may do none of the
above for the choice is entirely up to them.

11. See Philip Mitchell 'Medical and Psychological Aspects of Homosexuality'
in B.G.Webb (ed.) *Theological and Pastoral Responses to Homosexuality*, pp. 111-119.

Psychologists[12] working in the field have commented on the sense of difference that homosexual adolescents felt from their peers. Though possibly more apparent than real, this difference often involved physical characteristics. Specifically, they perceived themselves as less masculine or less feminine in appearance or physical attributes.

Perhaps the most generous position that could be put is that there may be biological influences at work in the causation of homosexuality, that are possibly to do with the way the individual perceives themselves and therefore others.

12. See for example Van den Aardweg G.J.M. *The Battle for Normality* (San Francisco: Ignatius Press, 1997), pp. 53-55.

On homosexuality and change

Dr Trevor Hunter

*I*n August 1997, the American Psychological Association, with a constituency of some 150,000 members, voted to brand as unethical any attempt by one of its members to attempt change in the sexuality of a client.

This was not a sudden step, but followed in accord with the American Psychiatric Association decision to delete homosexuality from its Diagnostic and Statistical Manual of Psychiatric Disorders (DSM-3), reclassifying it as a lifestyle choice rather than a behavioural or psychological disorder.

There are now no official voices willing to speak on homosexuality with regard to its causation or therapy in the North American continent. A lamentable situation, when you consider the cry for help seen in a letter published in *The Los*

Angeles Times earlier that year to one of its advice columnists.

Dear.........,

For the past few months I have been thinking seriously
about killing myself. I have tried to think of reasons not
to and the only one I come up with is that it would cause
my family lots of grief.

I am fifteen years old and feel so alone. I am scared
and I feel worthless. The problem is that I am absolutely
certain I am gay. At 15 a guy should be thinking about
what he wants to do in life, not how to end it. I have
always wanted to get married and have children but now
I know that life long dream is impossible. If there were
some pill to make all these sexual desires go away I
would gladly take it.

This isn't the easiest of letters to write and I have nobody
to talk to. Please help me as I cannot go on this way
much longer.[1]

The advice columnist was predictable in offering him no hope
or help to change.

Homosexuals are born, not made. They cannot change.
You must learn to accept yourself as you are.

She then recommended a pro-gay youth advocacy organisation
for him to contact. I suspect these words came to the boy as a
death knell, rather than as words of hope and life.

The situation elsewhere is not much better. *The Weekend
Australian* on 18th August, 1997, reported the rejection of

1.   *Los Angeles Times*, weekend 25th May, 1997.

funding by the Federal Government for an anti-suicide poster campaign directed at young people at risk because of homosexual feelings. The thrust of the campaign was for youth to accept their feelings, and join a support group. The campaign was developed by the West Australian AIDS Council in conjunction with The West Australian Gay and Lesbian Counselling Service, and urged young homosexuals to "trust their feelings". The Family Services Minister, Judi Moylan, rejected it on the basis that it leant towards "promoting a gay and lesbian lifestyle" rather than "identifying and protecting those at risk of suicide". Her decision was labelled as "appalling" and one that would *cost lives* " according to homosexual lobby groups.

It was in order to counter the message and themes of the pro-gay lobby, as demonstrated above, that a group of North American psychologists and psychiatrists have come together to form the National Association for the Research and Treatment of Homosexuality (NARTH).

An article on their work published in the *Wall Street Journal* commences with these words:

> Suppose a young man seeking help for a condition that was associated with serious health risks and made him desperately unhappy were to be told by the professional he consulted that no treatment were available, that his condition is genetic and permanent and that he must learn to live with it.
>
> How would he then feel were he to learn, perhaps years later, that numerous therapeutic approaches have been available for his specific problem for over 60 years? That though none of these approaches guaranteed results and most required a long period of treatment, if

accompanied by a strong motivation to change, there was a good chance of being free from that condition?

How then would he feel if he discovered that the reason he was not informed of his options was that certain groups were for political reasons pressuring professional groups to deny that effective treatment ever existed?[2]

NARTH has just released a collaborative study conducted over two years among 860 individuals seeking to overcome their homosexuality, and involved more than 200 psychologists and other therapists who have been treating them. The study was conducted by way of survey amongst the above groups, and the important features are noted below.

The study identified a group thought previously to be non-existent in the general population, those who experienced their homosexual feelings as unwanted and sought change.

Amongst the study's significant findings is a documented shift in respondents' sexual orientation, as well as the frequency and intensity of their homosexual thoughts and actions. Specifically the survey indicated:

1. Before treatment, 68% of respondents perceived themselves as exclusively or almost entirely homosexual, with another 22% saying they were more homosexual than heterosexual. After two years treatment only 13% perceived themselves as exclusively or entirely homosexual while 33% described themselves as either exclusively or almost entirely heterosexual.

2. Although only 83% of respondents indicated they had entered therapy primarily because of homosexuality, 99% of those who participated in the survey said they now believed treat-

2.   *Wall Street Journal*, January 9th, 1997.

ment to change homosexuality can be effective and valuable.

3. As a group, those surveyed reported statistically significant deceases following therapy in the frequency and intensity
of homosexual thoughts (63% prior to treatment to 3% after two
years), in the frequency of masturbation to homosexual pornography (42% to 2%), in the frequency of homosexual activity
with a partner (30% "very often" to 1%).

4. Of the therapists surveyed, 82% said they believed therapy
had changed their clients' orientation with, on average, one
third to one half of those clients adopting a primarily heterosexual orientation.

Of the primarily caucasian sample, 78% were men, 22%
women, with an average age of 37 years. Over half had never
married and about one third were married. 90% had a college
education.

Some comments from those surveyed

When I realised homosexuality was a trap I turned to
others for help. My therapist and our relationship provided a model for appropriate male to male non-sexual
relationships and taught me about appropriate touching, bonding and expression of need.

I have been involved in compulsive behaviour several
times a week for 8 years with physical encounters as
well. Since joining a therapy group I've had no recur-
rence of compulsive masturbation, no use of phone sex
or pornography and little desire to participate in those
things. The attraction to men lingers but every week I
participate (in) the group encourages me more.

A female respondent stated:

> I never expected this much recovery. My relationships
> with men have vastly improved—I am able to relate sex-
> ually to my husband in a way I was never able to before.
> I am learning to leave the protective emotions of contempt,
> arrogance, self-sufficiency, anger and self indulgence
> behind and practise the emotions of love instead.
>
> Change is extremely difficult and requires total com-
> mitment. But I have broken the terrible power that homo-
> sexuality had over me for so long. I haven't been this light
> and happy since I was a child. People can and do change.

Liberty and change

There is no indication from the study as to the Christian commitment of clients or therapists, though one could expect them
to figure in those seeking change or seeking to facilitate it. The
study would seem to give hope to all those wanting change. It is
valuable for organizations such as Liberty Christian Ministries,
who believe the gospel offers the dynamic for change for those
who seek it (1 Cor 6:9-11). Certainly a study as comprehensive as
this should put to rest the lie that change is impossible and any
attempt to seek change is doomed to failure.

While as a Christian organization Liberty can guarantee
nothing when it comes to the profoundly complex area of
human sexuality, yet by God's grace we refuse to exempt it from
the promises made to the individual when they turn to Christ.

> If anyone is in Christ, he is a new creation: the old has
> gone; the new has come! (2 Cor 5:17)

It seems impossible to believe that if a Christian seeks God's
grace to turn away from a dimension of their life which has

been a significant stumbling block that God will not be in their decision. For we know that sanctification is a work of God through his Spirit enacted in the life of the individual as he or she lives in obedience to the Word of God.

Liberty Christian Ministries Inc. seeks to facilitate the living of holy lives in the area of sexuality. For some, if not many, who are caught in the web of homosexuality, there is at least a way out—and the hope of much more as they continue to grow in the stature and image of Christ (2 Cor 3:16-18).

Homosexuality in the New Testament

Glenn N Davies

Summary

The evidence of the New Testament affirms the creation intentions for humanity as set forth in the Old Testament. Man and woman, as image bearers of God are created for sexual union in the context of marriage, which is the lifelong, exclusive union between a male and a female. While marriage is the norm, not everyone will enjoy the benefit of being married. Some will remain single, either by choice or circumstances. Moreover, the New Testament countenances no provision for any sexual activity outside of marriage, whether that activity be heterosexual or homosexual in nature. The prohibitions on homosexuality are not limited merely to cultic homosexuality or promiscuous homosexuality. Rather, Paul's condemnation of homosexual practice appears absolute. It is against nature for two women to be involved in sexual intercourse, as it is for two men. In fact,

Paul declares that such behaviour excludes one from an inheritance in the kingdom of God. However, this is not to suggest that homosexual behaviour is somehow more heinous than other sins. For all unrepented sin excludes one from God's kingdom. In this regard, homosexual activity is just one of a number of sins which are inconsistent and incompatible with the Christian life. The New Testament, accordingly, does not countenance the persecution of homosexuals that arises from a homophobia which does not recognise the validity and integrity of homosexuals as men and women made in the image of God.

However, it is not impossible, according to the apostle Paul, for homosexuals to change their behaviour. The homosexual, by God's grace, can be set free from their sin and sanctified in the name of the Lord Jesus and in the power of the Holy Sprit. There is hope for those who want to live God's way. Fidelity to the teaching of the New Testament will always extend hope and mercy to all those who love God and seek to keep his commandments.

Jesus

The teaching of the New Testament concerning sexuality assumes the understanding of marriage as the bond between a man and a woman, in accordance with the creation accounts of Genesis 1-2. Jesus' teaching on this subject reinforces the permanency and exclusivity of the sexual bond between a man and a woman (Matt 5:27-32; 19:1-12). Moreover, Jesus condemns all kinds of sexual impurity as evils to be avoided, including *porneiai* ('sexual immorality'), *moicheiai* ('adultery'), and *aselgeia* ('licentiousness') (Mark 7:20-23). The third term in this list suggests sexual licence or debauchery beyond the norm. Otto Bauernfeind suggests it characterises Sodom and Gomorrah (citing 2 Pet 2:7) and the pagan world generally (Eph 4:19), with a special sense of sexual excess (Rom 13:13; 2 Cor 12:21; 2 Pet 2:2,18).[1] Although it may not be possible to establish a specific reference to homosexual practice, the semantic range of *aselgeia* is inclusive of homosexual practice.

Jesus does not specifically address the question of homosexuality, but two points are worthy of attention. First, in the discussion of divorce in Matthew 19:1-12, the disciples' response to Jesus' high standards concerning marriage is to question whether it is better not to marry at all. However, Jesus' reply suggests that apart from marriage, the only other viable state is celibacy. Such celibacy may be the result of one being born a eunuch (the impotent), being made a eunuch (the castrated) or making a voluntary decision not to marry. It would therefore appear that Jesus did not contemplate homosexual union as a viable alternative of sexual expression for those who would be members of the kingdom of God. On the contrary, he reaffirmed and reinforced the teaching of the Old Testament with respect to sexual union (Matt 19:4-5; cf 5:17).

Second, Jesus affirmed loving relationships between his disciples. Apart from the oft-cited commandment to love one another (John 13:34), Jesus also evidenced a special love relationship with other men. Lazarus is described as one whom Jesus loved (John 11:36); a special relationship is evident between Jesus and the trio of Peter, James and John; and the author of John's Gospel also describes himself as the "disciple whom Jesus loved" (John 13:23; 19:26; 21:7; 21:20). Moreover, Jesus described his followers as "friends", suggesting a greater degree of intimacy than that conveyed by the term "servants" (John 15:15). Although there is no warrant to infer any sexual union by such descriptions of intimacy, it is important to note that the Gospel records do give ample testimony to the promotion of genuine, loving and caring

---

1. *The Dictionary of the New Testament*, 1.490.

relationships between people, beyond the marriage bond.[2]

Paul

When we turn to the Pauline writings, we find specific references to the practice of homosexuality, and in each instance the behaviour is viewed negatively. In Romans 1:26-27, Paul describes the kind of behaviour that is characteristic of the wicked, those who by their wickedness suppress the truth. The central concern of Paul's indictment of the wicked, however, is their rejection of God the creator. This rejection is exemplified by idolatry and results in God giving them up to all kinds of aberrant behaviour. Such behaviour includes a range of sins listed in verses 28-32, as well as that of homosexual practice discussed in verses 26-27. Homosexual behaviour therefore is not singled out above all others as worthy of special condemnation. Nonetheless, same-sex union is, according to the apostle, unnatural (*para physin*), where by way of contrast sexual relations between a man and a woman are natural (*physike*). In verse 26, Paul highlights the dishonour of sexual acts which are contrary to the created order of male/female relationships.[3] He first makes mention of sexual intercourse between females,[4] and then draws attention in greater detail to similar homosexual

2. The reference to the centurion whose servant was very dear (*entimos*) to him (Luke 7:2) is a reflection of the honour in which the centurion held his servant (or the value he was to him). However, it would be straining the text to consider that the description of "being dear" suggested the existence of a sexual relationship between the two men. Cf J. Duncan M. Derrett, *Law in the New Testament* (London: Darton, Longman & Todd, 1970), 174.
3. "The use of the adjectives meaning 'female' and 'male', rather than the words *gune* and *aner* is appropriate here, since it is the sexual differentiation as such on which attention is specially concentrated (cf. Gen 1:27; Mat 19:4=Mk 10:6; Gal 3:28)." Cranfield, 125.
4. The use of *chresis* for sexual relations is well attested (BAG, 894).

activity between men. Such same-sex activity is part of God's judgment upon the wicked, whether they be Jew or Gentile, in that they have rejected the one true God.

The depiction of homosexual activity as "against nature" (*para physin*) is, according to John Boswell, not a generalised statement about all homosexuality, but a reference to homosexual behaviour between heterosexual males.[5] For them it would be against nature, but not for those with a homosexual orientation. However, such a distinction is difficult to maintain in a first century world, which knew nothing of the concept of describing homosexuality as a condition as opposed to a behaviour (compare fornication or adultery). It is against nature because it is against God's created order for human beings ("contrary to the intentions of the creator", Cranfield, 125).[6] Similarly, despite the

5. J Boswell, *Christianity, Social Tolerance and Homosexuality* (Chicago: University Press, 1980), 110-12. L. William Countryman extends Boswell's thesis with a more detailed examination of the terminology of Romans 1:26-27, deducing that Paul is using same-sex union as an example of Gentile "uncleanness" which suggests a cultic distinction rather than a moral distinction. For a convincing rebuttal of this view see T. E. Schmidt, "Romans 1:26-27 – The Main Text in Context", *Striving for Gender Identity: Homosexuals and Christian Counseling. A Workbook for the Church*, ed. C. R. Vonholdt. Reichelsheim: Reichenberg Fellowship, 1996, 36-59. Cf R. B. Hays, "Relations Natural and Unnatural: A Response to John Boswell's Exegesis of Romans 1", *Journal of Religious Ethics* 14 (1986), 184-215; J. B. De Young, "The Meaning of 'Nature' in Romans 1 and its Implications for Biblical Perspectives of Homosexual Behavior", *JETS* 31 (1988), 429-47.
6. LSJ explain *para* as having three mains senses: I. *Beside, near, by;* II. *along;* III. *Past, beyond.* The idea of 'contrary to' is located under III. Their entries under III suggest a sequence of development along the lines: *past, beyond ... over and above ... in excess of ... in transgression of, in violation of.* This is similar to the idea of 'trans' in *transgress,* i.e., 'to go across/past/beyond the bounds of', etc. (Latin *trans* = *across*). Note Cranfield's reference to the use of *para* plus the accusative (in reference to v 25) as giving the meaning of "rather than", "in preference to", "instead of" (124). For further references to the use of *para physin* in contemporary literature, see the articles by Schmidt, Hays and De Young above.

attempts by some to deduce a philosophy of natural law, it is more likely that Paul was following the principles laid down in the Old Testament which prescribe marriage between a man and a woman as the only appropriate context for sexual union.

As B. G. Webb says:

> So *physis*, 'nature', in this context clearly denotes the world as God has made it, the created order. Paul has something more in mind than custom. He is appealing to what, in terms of the Bible's own theology, is prior to all culture: the will of God for human relationships expressed in the way he made us 'from the beginning' (Matt 19:4). Again we are back at Genesis 1-2.[7]

Nonetheless, it is also important to note that we all share in the fallenness of this present world order. For that reason, homosexual behaviour is not more heinous than other sins, which reflect the world in opposition to God. Accordingly, there is no justification for the persecution of such persons, who still bear the image of God, despite their sinful behaviour. As Helmut Thielicke so long ago observed:

> The predisposition itself, the homosexual potentiality as such, dare not be any more strongly depreciated than the status of existence which we *all* share as men in the disor-

7. B. G. Webb, "Homosexuality in Scripture", *Theological and Pastoral Responses to Homosexuality*, ed. B. G. Webb (Adelaide: Open Book, 1994), 87. Although J. A. Fitzmyer considers Paul's thinking to be coloured by Hellenistic philosophy, "in the context of vv. 19-23, 'nature' also expresses for him [Paul] the order intended by the Creator, the order seen in the function of sexual organs themselves, which were ordained for an expression of love between man and woman and for the procreation of children." *Romans* (New York/London: Doubleday, 1992), 286. See also the insightful analysis of G. Bahnsen, *Homosexuality: A Biblical View* (Grand Rapids: Baker, 1978), 53-61.

dered creation that exists since the Fall. Consequently, there is not the slightest excuse for maligning the constitutional homosexual morally or theologically. We are all under the same condemnation and each of us has received his "share" of it. In any case, from this point of view the homosexual share of that condemnation has no greater gravity which would justify any Pharisaic feelings of self-righteousness and integrity on the part of us "normal" persons.[8]

A second reference to homosexual practice is found in a catalogue of vices in 1 Corinthians 6:9-10. In this list Paul describes those persons who will be excluded from the kingdom of God. Such persons are generally described as the wicked or unrighteous (adikioi), and then specifically included are the sexually immoral (pornoi), adulterers (moichoi), male prostitutes (malakoi) and homosexual offenders (arsenokoitai). Gordon Fee comments:

The word malakoi has the basic meaning of 'soft' [cf Matt 11:8; Luke 7:25], but became a pejorative epithet for men who were 'soft' or 'effeminate', most likely referring to the younger, 'passive' partner in a pederastic relationship—the most common form of homosexuality in the Greco-Roman world.[9]

8. 12 H. Thielicke, The Ethics of Sex (tr J. W. Doberstein, London: James Clarke & Co., 1964), 283.
9. G. D. Fee, The First Epistle to the Corinthians (Grand Rapids: Eerdmans, 1987), 243; so also C. K. Barrett, A Commentary on the First Epistle to the Corinthians (New York: Harper & Row, 1980), 140. More generally, Dennis Prager states: "Indeed, for all intents and purposes, Judaism may be said to have invented the notion of homosexuality, for in the ancient world sexuality was not divided between heterosexuality and homosexuality. That division was the Bible's doing. Before the Bible, the world divided sexuality between penetrator (active partner) and penetrated (passive partner)." "Judaism's Sexual Revolution", Striving for Gender Identity: Homosexuals and Christian Counseling. A Workbook for the Church, ed. C. R .Vonholdt. (Reichelsheim: Reichenberg Fellowship, 1996), 17. See also Bahnsen, 50.

Yet, since *malakos* was not the usual word for such a person,[10] Fee admits to some difficulty in being certain of its designation in this list, if it were not for the appearance of the following word *arsenokoitai*.[11] This is the first time the word appears in preserved literature, and has most likely been coined by Paul to describe the sexual union of two males (cf. *arsenes en arsesin*, Rom 1:27): a compound of male and intercourse (literally 'bed').[12] The LXX of Leviticus 18:22 (*meta arsenos ou koimethese koiten gynaikeian*) is the most likely source for Paul's new word, which for both Old Testament Israel and new covenant Corinth was something to be avoided by the people of God. Although Paul does not reflect upon any homosexual orientation of the person as such, what he does make plain is that those who practise homosexual acts, along with those who practise other forms of sexual immorality,

10. The pejorative sense of the word has been found in a third century BC papyrus from Egypt (P. Hib. I (1906) 54, reproduced by A. Deissmann, *Light from the Ancient East* (tr L. R. M. Strachan; New York: G. H. Doran Co., 1927), 164.). In a letter from Demophon, a wealthy Egyptian, to Ptolemaeus, a police official, he writes: "Send us also Zenobius, the effeminate, with tabret and cymbals and rattles. For the women have need of him at the sacrifice." Deissmann comments: "The word [*malakos*=effeminate] is no doubt used in its secondary (obscene) use, as by St. Paul in 1 Cor 6:9. It is an allusion to the foul practices by which the musician eked out his earnings." In Modern Greek the word *malakos* also describes a person easily manipulated. However, the sexual connotations of the word group can be seen in the contemporary translations of *malakia* (masturbation) and *malaka* (wanker).

11. The 1946 edition of the RSV translated the two Greek words by the one English word "homosexuals", and in the second edition (1971) by the phrase "sexual perverts", whereas the NEB (1961) chose the phrase "homosexual perversion." Most other translations use two different words, e.g., "male prostitutes, homosexual offenders" (NIV); "self indulgent, sodomites" (JB); "male prostitutes, sodomites" (NRSV).

12. Note the use of the word *paidophthoros* ("corrupter of boys"), which while not used by the New Testament writers is found in Barnabas, Justin Martyr, Clement of Alexander and other classical writers.

will be excluded from the kingdom of God (1 Cor 6:10).[13] In a similar vein, Paul's instructions to Timothy indicate that the *arsenokoitai* (those who commit acts of homosexual behaviour) behave contrary to sound doctrine and contrary to the gospel (1 Tim 1:10-11). As Greg Bahnsen concludes:

> In ancient culture homosexuality was commonplace with certain distinctions customarily drawn between homosexuality as an ideal expression of love (e.g. in Plato's *Symposium*) or as an aid to military prowess (e.g., in Spartan propaganda) and homosexuality in the form of prostitution or indiscriminate infatuation. The one was encouraged, the other discouraged. By contrast, Paul, who was well versed in the culture of his day, drew no such distinctions but categorically condemned homosexuality without exception.[14]

Earlier in Paul's letter to the Corinthians (chapter 5), Paul wrote of his outrage upon hearing that one of the members of the congregation was living with his father's wife. Although Paul argues that such behaviour was not even found among the pagans, it is universally recognised that Paul's ethical stance is governed by the prohibitions of Leviticus 18:7-8. Such prohibitions are still in force under the new covenant.[15] Paul does not explore the level of commitment of the couple involved.

13. In Paul's extensive discussions concerning singleness, marriage and divorce in 1 Corinthians 7, it is clear that Paul, like Jesus, only contemplates two states of life: either as a married person, entailing an exclusive sexual union between husband and a wife; or as a single person, living a celibate life.

14. Bahnsen, 50.

15. The applicability of these prohibitions have long been recognised by Anglicans, as evidenced by the printing of the Table of Kindred and Affinity in the Book of Common Prayer.

He does not examine the evidence as to whether they truly love one another. In the face of such strong apostolic denunciation, there is no defence—it is condemned by God and requires the church to take action against it.

Nonetheless, it ought also to be noted that Paul does not consider that homosexual activity is so ingrained in a person's behaviour that there is no escape. The triune God is able to wash, sanctify and justify in the name of the Lord Jesus and by the Spirit of God. "That is what some of you *were*", Paul reminds the Corinthians (1 Cor 6:11). A history of homosexual behaviour, therefore, does not prevent a person from coming to Christ. Yet it is also true that homosexual behaviour should not continue for the person converted to Christ. This is not to suggest that such persons will be free from all temptations and inclinations to revert to homosexual conduct. However, as in all cases of temptation to sin, there is a way of escape for the disciple of Christ (1 Cor 10:13).[16]

Moreover, those who once took part in homosexual behaviour are not to be shunned because of their past offences. On the contrary, like all other sinners who have been saved by grace, they are to be welcomed as part of the body of Christ (Rom 15:7; 2 Cor 2:5-11).

16. Of course, knowing the way of escape and choosing it are not synonymous (Gal 5:16-26). However, the distinguishing mark of the Christian is that they recognise sin to be sin, even though they may still succumb to temptation. For a recent clinical approach to the opportunities of change for male homosexuals, see Joseph Nicolosi, *Reparative Therapy of Male Homosexuality: A New Clinical Approach* (Northvale, NJ/London: Jason Aronson Inc, 1997).

Jude

The reference to *sarkos heteras* (lit. 'other flesh') in Jude 7 could, as it has been argued by John Dunnill above, refer to miscegenation, the (unnatural) union of angels and humans. However, one cannot be dogmatic about this interpretation. Apart from alternative interpretations of Genesis 6:4, it is to be noted that Jude accuses not only Sodom of "other flesh" activity, but also the surrounding towns. Even if the sin of the city of Sodom was an attempt to have intercourse with angels (did they know of the angelic origin of these strangers?), we are hard pressed to find evidence of angel/human union occurring in the surrounding towns. Moreover, the men of Sodom did not have intercourse with the angels. Certainly there was the sin of lack of hospitality, but it is also the sin of sexual immorality (*ekporneuein*), embracing a wide range of sexual misconduct, which is condemned by the writer. Nonetheless, if Jude had wanted to single out homosexual activity as a specific sin he could easily have done so by the use of a more specific word. The fact that he did not, prevents us from drawing any specific application from this text to the issue of homosexuality. All that can be said is that sexual immorality was part of the sin of the city of Sodom, who thereby serve as an example of those who suffer the punishment of eternal fire (cf. 2 Pet 2:6).

Conclusion

The teaching of the New Testament concerning sexual union between humans is consistent with the teaching of the Old Testament. The male-female union within the bond of marriage is the only sexual union sanctioned by God. The New Testament writers regularly cite occurrences of sexual immorality in the Old Testament as behaviour to be avoided. However, within this strict moral guideline, the New Testament also acknowledges the weakness of the flesh and the power of God's grace. While homosexual activity is clearly described by the apostle Paul as sin, it is not the only sin, nor the worst sin. There is no justification, therefore, in persecuting homosexuals in the name of Christian piety.

Christians will never be free from sin in this world. Occasions of homosexual behaviour, do not therefore, exclude one from the kingdom of God any more than occasions of theft or murder. What is imperative for the Christian, however, is the acknowledgment that such acts are sinful and deserve God's judgment. Unless they repent of all sinful activity, they will be excluded from the kingdom of God. God's grace is sufficient to renew and sanctify all who turn to Christ, even those who fall into sin, time and time again. However, for those who choose to disobey God's commandments wilfully and deliberately, there no longer remains a sacrifice for sins (Heb 10:26). The Christian faith will be true to the New Testament when it affirms both the purity of God's ways and the forgiveness that is available to those who truly repent.

Bibliography

Bahnsen, G *Homosexuality: A Biblical View*. Grand Rapids: Baker, 1978.

Boswell, J *Christianity, Social Tolerance and Homosexuality*. Chicago: University Press, 1980.

Countryman, L W *Dirt, Greed and Sex*. Philadelphia: Fortress, 1988.

Cranfield, C E B *A Critical and Exegetical Commentary on the Epistle to the Romans, vol 1*. ICC; Edinburgh: T & T Clark, 1975.

De Young, J B "The Meaning of 'Nature' in Romans 1 and its
Implications for Biblical Perspectives of Homosexual Behavior", *JETS* 31
(1988), 429-47.

Fee, G D *The First Epistle to the Corinthians*. NIC; Grand Rapids:
Eerdmans, 1987.

Fitzmyer, J A *Romans*. Anchor Bible; New York/London: Doubleday,
1992.

Hays R B "Relations Natural and Unnatural: A Response to John
Boswell's Exegesis of Romans 1", *Journal of Religious Ethics* 14 (1986),
184-215.

Nicolosi, J *Reparative Therapy of Male Homosexuality: A New Clinical
Approach* Northvale, NJ/London: Jason Aronson Inc,, 1997.

Prager, D "Judaism's Sexual Revolution", *Striving for Gender Identity:
Homosexuals and Christian Counseling. A Workbook for the Church*, ed.
C R Vonholdt. Reichelsheim: Reichenberg Fellowship, 1996, 14-27.

Schmidt, T E "Romans 1:26-27 – The Main Text in Context", *Striving
for Gender Identity: Homosexuals and Christian Counseling. A Workbook
for the Church*, ed. C R Vonholdt. Reichelsheim: Reichenberg
Fellowship, 1996, 36-59.

Schmidt, T E *Straight and Narrow? Compassion and Clarity in the
Homosexuality Debate*. Leicester: IVP, 1995.

Scroggs, R *The New Testament and Homosexuality. Contextual Background
for Contemporary Debate*. Philadelphia: Fortress, 1983.

Thielicke, H *The Ethics of Sex*, tr J W Doberstein. London: James
Clarke & Co., 1964.

Webb, B G "Homosexuality in Scripture", *Theological and Pastoral
Responses to Homosexuality*. Explorations 8. Adelaide: Openbook, 1994,
65-103.

Wold, D J *Out of Order. Homosexuality in the Bible and the Ancient Near
East*. Grand Rapids: Baker, 1998.

Contact Details

Australia

Liberty Christian Ministries Inc.
PO Box 67
Summer Hill NSW 2130
Australia
Telephone (02) 9798 4685

Brisbane
Liberty Inc.
Telephone: 07 3390 4250
Email: libertyinc2083@aol.com
PO Box 2083
Tingalpa QLD 4173

Canberra
The Recovery Line
Telephone: 02 6291 7792
PO Box 1321
Fyshwick ACT 2609

Melbourne
Purple Heart
Telephone: 03 9699 2254
Email: purpleheart@access.net.au
PO Box 105
South Melbourne VIC 3205

International

Exodus Asia Pacific
PO Box 1882
Milton QLD 4064
Telephone: 07 3371 4705
Email: exodus@itconnect.net.au

True Freedom Trust
PO Box 13,
Prenton Wirral. CH43 6YB
Telephone 0151 653 0773
Fax 0151 653 7036
Email<martin@tftrust u-net com>
http://www.tftrust.u-net.com/

Exodus International North America
PO Box 77652,
Seattle, WA 98177.
Phone: 206/ 784-7799.
Fax: 206/ 784-7872
Internet: http://www.
exodusnorthamerica.org

Exodus will supply contact names
of Christian Ministries for people
wishing to deal with unwanted
homosexual feelings worldwide.

What some of you were...

study guide

—— Three discussions for small groups ——

Discussion 1: Understanding homosexuality

Read the section 'Our stories' and the article 'Is homosexuality biologically determined?' before coming to the group.

In the group, read Genesis 1:26-31, 2:18-23 and Galatians 5:16-26. As you read, consider these questions:

What were humans created to be? How has this changed?

Are we forced to live according to the desires of our nature?

Discuss some of these questions:

1. What is homosexuality? What are some of its causes?

2. What is often missing in the childhood or family background of men and women with homosexual feelings?

3. What struck you about the struggles of some of the people in these stories?

4. Is gayness biologically determined? What difference would it make if it were?

5. What is the difference between the causes of our behaviour and our personal responsibility for behaviour?

6. How does the Bible's teaching about creation affect our attitudes towards human nature and personal responsibility?

Pray: for all those struggling with feelings of same-sex attraction, that God might change them.

Discussion 2: Homosexuality in the church

Read the sections 'mother', 'daughter' and 'wife' before coming to the group.

In the group, read 1 Cor 6:9-11. Consider:
Are all these sins equally bad?
What is the right response to each of these sins?

Discuss some of these questions:

1. What struck you about the reactions of these people when they were told of the feelings of their family member? How do you think you would react?

2. What struck you as the most helpful reaction in the stories? Why do you think it was helpful?

3. Imagine the scenario when you find there is someone in your church who has been actively gay but wants to conform to Christ. What sort of things could you do to help? Would you be prepared to do these things? What if it was your close friend?

4. What about someone who had feelings of same-sex attraction but was not active?

Pray: for churches, that they might help those struggling with homosexuality and support Christian brothers and sisters in the best way.

Discussion 3: Homosexuality outside the church

Read the chapters 'How we went gay', 'Homosexuality in the New Testament' and 'On homosexuality and change' before coming to the group.

In the group, look at these passages and for each passage answer:
> What do we learn about sexual relations?
> What reasons are there for not having homosexual or extra-marital sex?

Genesis 2:18-25; Leviticus 18:22-24 and 20:13 (read a few surrounding verses for context); Romans 1:18-32.

Discuss some of these questions:

1. What do you think of the statement "AIDS is not God's judgement on homosexuality; homosexuality is God's judgement on idolatry"?

2. How can we speak truthfully about homosexuality in today's world, without being homophobic?

3. Why has our society accepted the gay movement?

4. What might be some good ways for Christians to react to the gay movement in society at large?

Pray: for our witness to the wider world, in making God's word of judgement and forgiveness clear.

Other books from Matthias Media...

Pure Sex

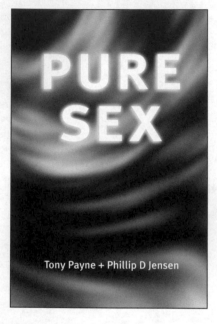

Phillip Jensen and Tony Payne take a look at what the Bible teaches about sex, and at what this means in the sexual climate of the new millennium. In doing so, they give Christians clear and compelling reasons for standing apart and being different from the world around them; but they also provide a challenge to the non-Christian person who realises that something is very wrong with the model of sexuality we are now living with, post the sexual revolution.

This compelling book shows how our society has come to hold such a confused and destructive view of sex, and why the Bible's alternative is so liberating.

ORDERING DETAILS:

United Kingdom

The Good Book Company
Telephone: 0845 225 0880
Facsimile: 0845 225 0990
Email: admin@thegoodbook.co.uk

www.thegoodbook.co.uk

The Essence of Feminism

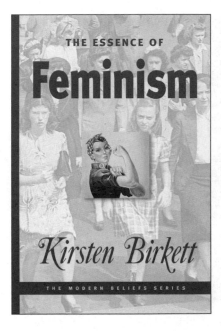

Feminism has permeated the modern world—it affects how we act, how we think, how we speak. It is one of the most powerful forces in Western society. How did it get to be that way? Are its claims true and are its arguments valid?

In this new book, Kirsten Birkett has researched the origins of modern feminism, what it fought for and what it has achieved. She began writing the book considering herself a feminist. By the end, she was no longer one and this book explains why.

The Essence of Feminism is certain to challenge and educate its readers. It is required reading for anyone seeking to understand and respond to the most significant social movement of our generation.

ORDERING DETAILS:

United Kingdom

The Good Book Company
Telephone: 0845 225 0880
Facsimile: 0845 225 0990
Email: admin@thegoodbook.co.uk

www.thegoodbook.co.uk

A Fresh Start

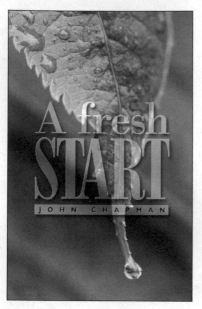

John Chapman's clear, persuasive and engaging presentation of the good news of Jesus is as fresh and readable as ever.

The book gives a straightforward explanation of our problem before God, his solution, how we can know it is all true, and what we should do about it.

Highly recommended.

United Kingdom

The Good Book Company
Telephone: 0845 225 0880
Facsimile: 0845 225 0990
Email: admin@thegoodbook.co.uk

www.thegoodbook.co.uk